D1736114

Nancy,

OK, LITTLE BIRD

Nice to have met t &
hope you find joy, laughter
+ inspiration in the story!
Elen

OK, LITTLE BIRD

a father-daughter memoir

DEENA GOLDSTEIN

OK, Little Bird
A Father-Daughter Memoir

Library of Congress Cataloging-in-Publication Data
Names: Goldstein, Deena, author.
Title: OK, Little Bird: A Father-Daughter Memoir
Description: First Edition | BookBaby 2021

ISBN 978-1-66781-8-108 (Print) | ISBN 978-1-66781-8-115 (eBook)

Designed and Published by BookBaby.
www.bookbaby.com
First Edition
Printed in the United States of America

For Dad, I love you.

Contents

Prologue

Whenever I visit the cemetery, I often wonder what my father would say to me from, as he would put it, "the other side of the grass." Given his propensity to gripe about anything and everything, I imagine it would be something like this: "Jesus Christ, it's cold down here! For what we paid for this casket, you'd think they could have used a warmer lining! Freakin' sprinklers! Surprised I haven't floated out to the highway yet! Every ten minutes the goddamn sprinklers are going off. Now I hear light footsteps coming down the path. Wonder who it … Deena? It's Deena! Hi, honey! What I would give to let her know I see her, hear her, and love her from beyond."

I always felt such a dichotomy between the loving words of advice my father gave me and the unsolicited advice and commentaries I was often privy to. There was the time I was still in my twenties, off to make my mark in the world. Far from self-assured yet a little scared. I gripped a neatly folded twenty-dollar bill and a letter as I embarked on a plane to Chicago. I glanced over my shoulder to catch my father's love-filled eyes as he waved one last time. "Don't read this till you're on the plane," he had said before handing me the envelope. "The twenty is for your cab—a little something from me." My father's letter held all the support, love, and faith that I would succeed.

My father's letter was a paper microcosm of all the love and support he provided me with while I was growing up. Whether I was squeaking out cacophonous screeches on my violin, exhibiting my artwork, or just needed a shoulder to lean on, he was there always, without question or judgment. A best friend to banter with, laugh and gain a little advice here and there.

My father implored me that I stay exactly as I was. "Don't change. You're perfect the way you are." Without him here, I don't feel perfect. At times, it's as if I can't feel at all.

My father was bigger than life and made life bigger for me. I was granted access into the inner sanctum of my father's emotions, humor, and softer side.

I can't remember a time in my life when I wasn't soaring with joy, lightness and the dawn of a new day with my dad, until the unthinkable happened, and I found out he wasn't invincible. There is no preparedness manual for a separation that removes the breath from your lungs. There is no guide to filling in spaces that can only be filled by the very person who no longer exists.

My father may have departed this world, but he left behind his love and an irreverent prescription for life. I'm tasked with carrying his flaming torch of witticisms, commentaries on underbaked muffins and stylish loafers, his well-honed craft of consuming donuts, pudding and poorly made sub sandwiches, while simultaneously complaining about them. I'll continue to make his signature faces, check my shoes for unsightly scuffs and seek out the best deal on a fabulous shirt.

Mostly, I'll continue down the path he set me on of self-sufficiency, doing the right thing, working hard, loving, being a good parent, a loyal friend and a good human. And, as genetics would have it, his stunt double. His story has not ended, it continues with me (and our entire family). I have the joy of sharing parts only I was witness to because I impishly wriggled my way into his stern and tough-skinned heart. The more I pushed, the more he laughed and loved, even when his gripes and commentaries continued.

"Hi, Dad!"

"Hi, Deena."

"What are you doing?"

"What am I *doing*? I'm watching a movie. Is that why you called?"

"Well, no. I just wanted to say hi. What's new? What movie are you watching?"

"Nothing's new. Everything's the same as the last time I talked to you, which was yesterday, by the way. I'm watching some old movie I've seen a hundred times. Sorry, honey, not in the mood to kibbitz."

"OK, well, I just was thinking about you and wanted to say hi."

"Well, OK, Deena. I'm hanging up now. I always love hearing from you. I just want to watch my show!"

I am the youngest of three children. Upon my arrival into this world, without question or consideration, I was deemed the "low girl on the totem pole." Things were humming quite nicely, before I came along. My low familial ranking meant nothing. From the moment I was born, my father and I shared a connection that singlehandedly changed our entire family dynamics and is the beginning of my story. It was love at first sight, and my father already knew things I didn't—like how much he would love me beyond all comprehension.

My father adored my sister, Andrea, and brother, Michael, but my mother would tell me that my father wished for an impish baby girl, with lots of dark hair. Looking back, I believe my father had thawed from some of his rigid parenting and was ready to have some fun. "God, I wish she were twins. Can you imagine two of her?" he'd often privately share with my mother. There was not one specific incident that fused our bond. I believe I was simply born at the right time—the time my father was ready to play.

My existence was as exciting to Andrea and Michael as getting cavities filled at the dentist. My brother recalls my mother entering the house with me bundled in her arms as she announced, "I brought you something."

My brother, excited at the prospect of a new toy, came running toward her. "What's this?" he asked.

"That's your new baby sister, Deena!" she joyfully told him.

I didn't bounce, race around like a toy car, or look like a football. Therefore, my brother turned on his heel disinterested. My sister, the oldest, sensed a newfound responsibility now added to her already growing list of responsibilities. Namely, watching over me (Andrea was 5 ½ years older and therefore my inescapable babysitter). Eventually, she would be relegated to watching over me and Michael, as we were constantly in a tangle of sibling chaos.

"If we did half the stuff Deena did, Dad would get so mad. How does she get away with it?!" Michael and Andrea would often infuriatingly share amongst themselves. Their expressions were often incredulous and frustrated when they watched my interactions with our father. As my entire family watched my relationship with my father play out through the years, they witnessed the impossible (shattering my father's crusty veneer) made possible by my unfiltered mouth and in-his-face approach.

It was no secret my father and I were connected in ways that my brother and sister, well, weren't. My mother would say that I brought my father joy nobody else in his life could. In later years, Michael and Andrea would verbalize the same sentiment. I had wormed my way into my father's heart and soul. The crazy thing is, I wasn't doing anything special. I was just being me. Dad found everything I did to be funny and was often charmed by my disregard for the barometric pressure of his temperament. I was rarely serious, and my lightness became endearing to him. My father thought I was a "character." As a toddler, when I did something I knew was wrong, I would run to my father and boldly declare, "I talked back to Mom, and I didn't finish my dinner, so I'm grounding myself, and going to my room without food." My father hid his hysteria behind his hand, as I turned on my heel to head to my self-inflicted punishment. Even in the usurpation of his parental powers, he remained amused.

I was a noisy chatterbox, unafraid to engage in conversation with my parents' friends, teachers, or other adults. In fact, I loved being around adults, as it was far more interesting and less filtered than being with my peers. The adults seemed to "get me." "Being seen and not heard" was not my anthem. My father said nothing, did nothing, and simply enjoyed my unbridled energy. In fact, he loved taking me with him everywhere for that very reason. "Sonny, can't you control her?" my father's father would say to him. My siblings would tell you it was as if I had been raised by a different father.

The absolute epitome of my unflinching willingness to weather my father's tsunami was when I asked him to buy me a hot pretzel after Sunday school—something Michael and Andrea would never try. "Deeeeenna," my father would whine, "really? You need a pretzel? How bad do you need a pretzel? There's a line. We'll have to wait, then there's going to be traffic."

Do you think this stopped me? Of course not! "Daaaaad, I reaaaalllly want a pretzel badly," I'd implore as I mounted the front seat console and got in his face. Eventually, I'd wear him down.

"OK, OK, hurry up. I've got cars crawling up my ass." And just like that, he would dig in his pocket for change, and I'd ride home with a salty hot pretzel while my brother and sister took turns quietly hating me.

And so began my life as the annoying little sister, the brat (as my sister coined me), or "pigface" (as my brother nicknamed me). This was an esteem-sucking title he gifted me due to my wee, upturned nose. I regarded Andrea as more of a parental figure than a playmate. Stealing gum from her purse, colluding with my brother on prank phone calls, or taking cookie dough while she was baking was all just pure aggravation to her. For the most part, she rightfully steered clear of me and my brother as often as possible.

As for my mother, while the relationship we had was great, it was just different than the one I had with Dad.

Sonny with a Chance of Suave

Born Maynard, in Dubois, Pennsylvania, my father began his life nicknamed "Sonny" by his family and friends. As a young man, despising the name Maynard and wanting separation from "Sonny," he knighted himself "Marc." My father's upbringing was fraught with the comingling of a strict home and an anti-Semitic neighborhood. In an essay he crafted in later years, he details his love of always wanting to be a cowboy like Roy Rogers or John Wayne in a shoot-'em-up spaghetti western. En route to and from school, he would be beaten up daily by Jew-hating neighbor boys. "There wasn't another Jew for miles; they hated us," he shared in the essay. When he wasn't in public school, he was learning Hebrew in preparation for his bar mitzvah. From the same essay, he recounts how he enjoys singing, acting in school productions, playing the trumpet, and being around people.

Maynard, an Academic student, was known to his friends as "Sonny." He was in the band, dance band, and broadcasters club his sophomore year. "Sonny" was a member of chorus for two years and dramatics club his senior year. He plans to enter U.C.L.A. or go to California to take up business.

The middle child of three, close with his mother and always under the microscope of his father's stringent expectations, my father was a prankster who liked to mess around with his younger brother, Aaron. "I always got him in trouble, and we had so much fun together!" he loved to say. At age ten, dad began working at his father's store, sweeping, washing windows, etc. At times, he worked with his brother Aaron at the store, where together they would always find time to have fun with one another under the radar of their father's scrutinizing sensibilities. His father, Robert ("Bob"), would offer unsolicited critical analysis of their behavior. Always a little hurt that he couldn't seem to get things "right" in his father's eyes, my dad always maintained a sense of humor about things.

He simply loved having fun.

Despite his plans to attend U.C.L.A., my father enlisted in the Navy (which many young men did then right after high school graduation), attending bootcamp in Bainbridge, Maryland, where he remained for fourteen weeks. Following bootcamp, he found himself at the US Naval Hospital Corps in Portsmouth, Virginia, where he was provided intensified medical training in pharmacology, toxicology, first aid, anatomy, physiology, minor surgery, nursing care, and self-preservation in atomic warfare. The training was brief in scope and gave him the designation of Navy Medic. He would share tales of taking blood pressure readings, administering injections, and dispensing medication to his fellow service buddies. "Deena, do you know the name for a blood pressure cuff?" he'd love to ask me.

"No, what is it?" I'd excitedly reply. (I loved when he taught me things.)

"Sphygmomanometer," he slowly and carefully replied.

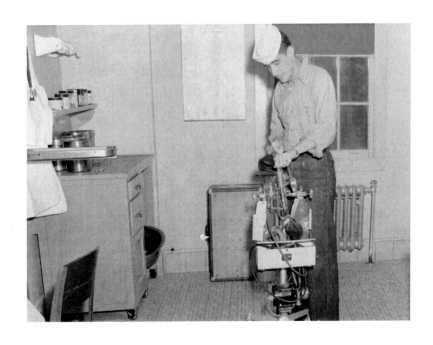

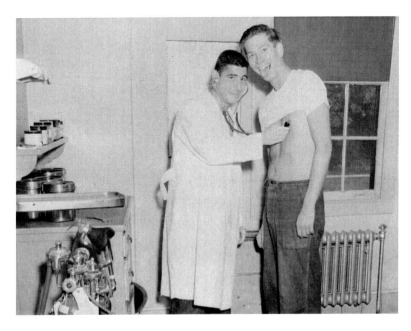

"Sphygmomimometer . . . sphymoomeeeter . . ." I'd bumble. Dad would laugh and continue to quiz me until I learned the correct pronunciation.

Following his short time in the Navy, he enrolled at the University of Michigan, attending only for a semester. While at Michigan, my father and mother were set up on a blind date. He arrived early, drank her beer and tossed her cat, Pitsicatto, out the window, after which they determined they would either hate each other or get married. She was beautiful, smart, independent, and saw through his antics. Marriage it was, and so Dad felt he needed to start earning a living, so he left school.

My father had an amazing sense of humor and was always cracking jokes with anyone who would listen. He was a ham. When he was provided a microphone and audience at sales meetings, weddings, or other life events, Dad brought the room to fits of laughter with the effortless ease of a seasoned comic. For a brief period, we had a home karaoke unit, and Dad loved to grab the microphone to sing Johnny Cash's "Burning Ring of Fire" any chance he got.

Dad was bright, bighearted, handsome, a snappy dresser, playful, and *stern*! His closet was replete with a wardrobe of his beloved cowboy attire and enough belts and cowboy boots to open a store. My father's love of all things Western began when he was a kid, but his dreams of becoming a horseback riding cowboy, like those he idolized in spaghetti Westerns, came to fruition when his close friend asked him to join him for a horseback ride. Suddenly, my father was now riding down his own dusty trail. He loved it! Following the ride, my father and some of his mutual friends invested in local horse property. Dad was so entrenched in his world of horses that he announced his early retirement and took leave of the business he shared with his brother and partners, so he could spend his days at the stable, selling tack and helping to facilitate horseback riding instruction and the eventual acquisition of additional horse properties. He spent a lot of time researching and acquiring his own horse, as well as grooming and trail riding. When my father wasn't near or on a horse, he could most surely be found discussing the acquisition of his next love: a new car.

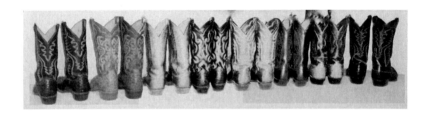

My father loved cars and the "art of the deal." During my child-hood, it would not be unusual to accompany my father to a car dealer-ship where he would schmooze with the car salesman, touch, and feel the smooth, supple leather of his soon-to-be vehicle and work a deal. And my father always worked a good deal! He knew oodles about car leasing, and his blunt force approach nearly always got him what he wanted, including a free hat! "Deena," he'd tell me, "you gotta ask for what you want. Know your information and numbers before you go in, so they won't take advantage of you. I'm always happy to go with you, but if I can't, you'll be able to do just fine. Always make them throw in mats and an oil change for free. You're spending a lot of money. It costs them almost nothing." (On all my car purchases and leases, I've always worked car mats and free oil changes into the deal.) Eventually, Michael and Andrea both became successful entrepreneurs. Michael took my father's "art of the deal" to a new level, and has been uber-successful in his many business start-ups and ventures.

The strict rules my father grew up with in a conservative Jewish home became the rules of our home. Manners, pressed clothes, not speaking unless spoken too, and an always respectful disposition were tenets of my father's childhood. Our home was much the same. *Wash your hands. Sit up straight. Keep your elbows off the table during mealtime. Chew with your mouth closed. Don't chew gum or eat in my car. Wash your neck.* None of us knew exactly how you soil your neck, but we were not permitted at the dinner table without our necks shining like the top of the Chrysler building. (Apparently, I was the worst offender as far as neck filth was concerned.) Watchful of my father's unyielding rules, Andrea, Michael, and I could have easily been accepted into any military academy with honors! If one of us sauntered in front of Dad during the 6 o'clock news, shoved excessive fistfuls of food in our mouths, or asked him for anything, he mostly surely would have opened a can of borscht whoop ass on us. For all his crank and grumbling, he was truly all bark and no bite.

Asking my father for things incited fear in his progeny. My father was not violent, and he wasn't profane, but it was his malleable, ever-changing facial expressions and irritable moods that would elicit trepidation and the need to locate the nearest exit. My father's eyebrows and nostrils would contort themselves in ways we had not known possible. In Yiddish, we affectionately referred to this as "challishing" (Jewish households morph their own Yiddish-isms, and this was ours.) Although my father could come across as a misanthrope due to his unfiltered, disparaging remarks, his perfectionism and finicky tastes were byproducts of his upbringing and the expectations placed on him by his father. If you were not privy to his past, you would simply take him at face value. Those that knew him well had a deeper under-standing and appreciation for who he was: a super irritable, really lovable curmudgeon.

As a licensed psychotherapist, my mother, Joan, knew to ignore my father's "Mr. Potato Head" facial contortions and dark moods. She had a way of seeing the brighter side of everything, including my father. They had a choreographed dance, well-honed and understood by only them. They loved each other deeply and through it all, never missed an opportunity to argue when in a moving vehicle or partake in heated controversy over the spatial relations of loading a trunk (my mother was always right, despite my dad arguing his point until his ego was zapped). Throughout the years, she was able to navigate the curmud-geon-infested waters with a smile on her face and spring in her step. My mother would share with me in later years that understanding my father's upbringing helped her understand and react to who he was. My father was most definitely a product of his father's rigid, unflinching rules, and his constant reprehension at anything he did. In other words, nothing my father could do was good enough in his father's eyes. This would forever quietly haunt him and form the protective layer that kept his softness at bay in his later years. My mother's professional background provided her with boundless patience and clarity. Her unconditional love provided the rest. She was able to depersonalize most of my father's stormy, unpredictable nonsense. She would say that together; they were yin and yang. My father was truly a kind, bright man, a loyal friend, and well-meaning soul. His irreverent sense of humor seeped through his tough exterior, which although off-putting, was more to protect himself, then offend.

Liver with a Side
of Common-tater
and Other Tales
from Hell's Kitchen

Essentially, each member of the family learned how to navigate my father's temperament in his or her own way. My sister, Andrea, the eldest, sought escape routes to her room or would avoid one-on-one encounters with my father, who, although he loved her dearly, was habitually critical of her. My brother, Michael, the second oldest, was very sensitive, but even at a young age, like an attorney arguing his points, would stay in the throws to show how he was towing the line. And me, I watched my father's interactions with my siblings, made myself quietly invisible during moments of contention, and then pounced into my father's lap, getting up close to his face. My "up close and personal" facial games morphed into "Owl," a wonderful exchange he and I did for years to come. Nose to nose, with our eyes shut, he'd say, "Now, one, two, three, open your eyes!" (My father did this with my daughter when she was growing up as well.) I felt no fear or intimidation. I was an extremely happy child, so I could not understand or relate to anything or anyone who was not equally as jubilant. When my father lacked joy, I literally eclipsed his personal space until he smiled. And he always did.

What was it about asking my father for anything that caused such disdain? He would instantly become frustrated if he was called upon to do literally anything that involved what I like to call effort. Getting up, changing the channel, picking up milk at the store—anything that exerted energy (with the exception of riding a horse) was off the table. (More on horses to come.)

Needless to say, the ambience in my house was strictly tow-the-line. At nightly dinners, my father would typically unleash a verbal firing squad at my sister who, through no fault of her own, and her biochemistry, would exhibit nervous physical movements. My father, at that unevolved point in his life, lacked the ability to deal with anything challenging his righteous expectations, particularly behaviors he couldn't control. Andrea's nerves manifested in a variety of ways and none of them fell into the "acceptable" category for him, so therein began his attempts to stop or change what she was doing through his perpetual critiques. "Andrea, sit *still!*" It was staggering to me that he believed he could somehow change what my sister was powerless to control. My father, criticized by his father, unleashed on her the very criticism he loathed. His father sought perfection in him, and therefore he sought perfection in my sister (and many people and things in his environment). (Ironically, I always thought my sister *was* perfect.) Seemingly simple things like carrots were the bane of our culinary existence, as they became veritable decibel bombs to my father even when we chewed with our mouths closed! My brother would become a target if he swung his legs under the table, which usually provoked him into whispering insults across the table at me. Like a passing of the torch, Dad would chastise Michael, and Michael would catch my eye and whisper, "You're a pigface," to me. His inaudible slights angered me so much that I'd implore him to stop at the top of my lungs. Needless to say, my father was not happy with my "shrill" cry for help. Where I was concerned, my only job at dinner was to arrive at the table with clean hands and neck and napkin in lap. In our estimation, paper napkins were most certainly not just for dainty mouth blotting; they were for poking holes into—another thing that maddened my father.

I didn't always escape my father's scrutiny, as due to auditory issues, I often spoke very loudly. As a toddler, I had chronic issues with fluid build-up in my ears and had repeated surgeries to drain and correct this situation. Through the course of many surgical procedures, I suffered mild hearing loss and ended up with challenges modulating my voice. "Deena, you're shrieking in my ear. I'm sitting right here. Talk quieter!" Dad would angrily spout. This was usually accompanied by a less than endearing facial expression that momentarily twisted my insides. I have memories of his father (my grandfather), who wore a hearing aid, annoyed with the decibel of my voice. He'd say to my father as he adjusted his hearing aid, "She's so shrill. Can't you get her to quiet down?" The timber and pitch of my voice was always a touchy subject for me. I felt unlovable and understood how my sister must have felt for things she also couldn't control. I was also known for poorly timed outbursts of laughter after which I'd be sent from the table until I could "act like a human being." In typical Deena fashion, I'd return to the table and burst out laughing again. Ultimately, my father did nothing.

In a nutshell, dinnertime was unpleasant. Our food stuck in our gullets like paste. We were grateful for our Great Dane, Buffy, who made it appear as if we had "cleaned our plates." Feeding Buffy helped expedite a speedy exit and end to the dinner hour, especially when liver was served. (What book advised parents to serve organ meat to their children, I'll never know.) Buffy became so accustomed to "de-liver-ies" under the kitchen table that regular dog food was a second thought. On Sundays, our family had a brief respite from liver-induced stress with hotdog night which consisted of beans, a small sampling of cold, effervescing Pepsi, potato chips, and my father's favorite, kosher knockwursts. Something about hotdog night was exciting, even though what preceded it had a depressive quality with my father napping on the couch, shades drawn. The only light source in the room came from his beloved television set. My mother would shout, "Go wake your father. It's time for dinner!" None of us wanted to be appointed to this task. "Deena, you do it!" Andrea and Michael begged. And I did. With regard to dessert, it was never served "at" the table. It was a cookie jar "free for all." "Deena, what are you doing in there?" Dad would yell from the family room as I tried to extract a cookie. Eventually, I honed my Houdini cookie trick and would dash off to eat it somewhere unnoticed.

Nobody messed with my father—except me. I don't know what it was that gave me the idea I could somehow penetrate his steely veneer, but at my earliest age, I can remember getting in his face to provide distraction, or anything that would draw his happy side out. My siblings would watch slack jawed as I poked the proverbial tiger. Their concern was not for me; it was for the potential repercussions that could ultimately affect them. Whether I was doing voice impersonations of his favorite movie stars (such as John Wayne, Jimmy Stewart), sidling up to him on the couch, or making silly faces, ultimately, he would laugh it off and any irritability was diffused, at least for me. Therefore, I never stopped trying, and my father never made me stop. I was the only person in my father's orbit that his irritability didn't yield power over, and he loved it. Michael and Andrea would become enraged at the sheer inequality and grace they were clearly not extended.

My father and I had diametrically opposed dispositions. I could be happy, and he could be irritable. He could be impatient, and I could be tolerant for an eternity. I believe our dissimilarities created our bond. Despite all his gruffness and grumbly exterior, there lived a kind, loving soul within him. We all somehow knew this, but what we experienced was what we individually reacted to. I would come to learn from my mother that I was the only person he let his guard down with. My father's humor was a window to an untapped universe of lightness that even he was unable to access with any regularity. Even under the worst of circumstances, I could always make my father laugh. We danced a dance that was like no other. Our relationship had its own rhythm and synchronicity. Pure love, fun, and utter joy always passed between us. His warm, gravelly voice and silly antics were home. We shared an indescribable bond of trust, acceptance, and the ability to be playful with one another. He felt safe.

When my middle and high school grades were much less than perfect, my father patiently asked, "Was there something you could have done differently?" He understood schoolwork was a challenge, particularly math. And there were also my well-known talkative outbursts during class. "Deena, is there any chance you were talking in class?" he gently would inquire. Understanding there was a distinct possibility I was inattentive and socializing, he was always kind about how he broached the topic. He never shamed or made me feel badly about how hard school was for me.

I remember the time I was bullied into calling my teacher a "pink pig" in grade school, which culminated in the dispensing of so many detentions my teacher's wrist gave out writing them (You can't blame me. She had pink bauble earrings, pink lipstick and smelled like cigarettes and coffee.) I had a violin concert at school that evening. On the way home in the car, my dad was complimentary on my performance, but then he asked, "Deena, why are you so quiet back there. You're never this quiet. Is everything OK?"

"Well, I kind of got in trouble today," I softly replied.

Dad lightly chuckled. "Trouble, what kind of trouble?"

"Well, these girls at my table dared me to call the teacher a pink pig. And I did, but I yelled it across the classroom, and she got so mad that she wrote me a ton of detentions."

"Deena . . . !" Dad exclaimed while trying not to laugh at something he clearly thought was funny. "You know, just because people tell you to do something, doesn't mean you do it. Do you think you learned your lesson? Sounds like your mom is gonna need to go down to school and get you out of some of those detentions or she'll be chauffeuring you for months."

My father supported my spirit, my early love of art and drawing, and challenged me to keep trying when things got tough. Around age six, I began singing. I pranced and sang all over the house, and my father loved to watch me perform. I sang the same songs repeatedly, without reproach. My father purchased for me a "sing-a-long" toy, an early version of a mini-portable karaoke machine. "Delta Dawn, what's that flower you have on," I'd belt out in front of anyone. My father would ask, "Do you know any other songs?" Despite protestations from my siblings, I continued my repetitive vocals for years to come. "You could be a country singer when you grow up, Deena," Dad said to me. Loud and occasionally off key, he made me feel my imperfections were perfect. We filled up each other's proverbial empty spaces, that somehow, we knew needed filling.

When my father mentioned wanting or needing something, I had it at his doorstep.

"Hey Dee, would you mind bringing me some Excedrin and a glass of ice water? I've been on the road all day for work, and I have a bad headache." I quickly became my father's headache reliever, paper delivery girl, channel changer, and foot rubbing assistant. And I loved every minute of it, as these small offerings brought him visible relief. When I knew he was feeling sad, I sat with him in silence. In my teens when his father died, we held hands in the large, glass paned, hospital vestibule. I took him to medical appointments, out to lunch and to get his hearing aids calibrated. When he was horrified at his appearance due to extreme weight loss from illness, he allowed me to assist him in putting his shirt on following a medical procedure. "I'm so embarrassed, Deena. Jesus, I look like a stick." And this proud man, so humiliated by his appearance which meant so much to him, allowed me to be witness to his vulnerability.

From my earliest childhood memories, I can recall lighting up at my father's entrance into a room. Whether he was picking me up from school, coming home from work, or sitting through one of my cacophonous violin performances, he was always the center of my universe. The feeling was mutual. Whether I was visiting my father at his office, stopping by his lunch with the guys, he always beamed, and my heart fluttered as he introduced me as his "baby girl." Each time, I thought I'd burst with joy. Plainly stated, we were lifetime members of our own mutual fan club.

My father's perpetual pride in me served up an abundance of confidence and joy. We were always excited to see one another, as if for the first time. The excitement that passed between us was a love that never wavered or changed based on stormy moods, tempers, or life events. My father may have been stern, but his steely veneer was as tough as the skin on a paper kite, tough enough to fly, but delicate enough to be torn. I was able to see through him always, and together we would take flight, tears in the kite and all.

When we weren't laughing, we were able to be comfortably silent with one another. We did life together. There were family events, celebrations, dinners, errands, and milestones, like the birth of my daughter. My father recently passed, and this memoir is a result of gathering these experiences and defining moments that tell our story. These snippets are fractals of time, which form the entity of who we once were.

The Hospice Time Machine

A heavy quiet fills the room. A silence filled with the sounds of slowing respiration and life, my father's life. I sit like a jackal guarding an Egyptian pharaoh's tomb. Despite my vigilance, I'm helpless in staving off what's to come.

I remain as close to my father's side as I have my entire life. The only difference now is that I'm seated next to his bed in a group home, rather than next to him on his favorite part of the couch at home. In January of 2020, my father celebrated his 85th birthday; however, following what seemed his last burst of life among family and friends and a veritable goodbye party, his health dramatically declined. Based on the 24-hour medical care he required, my mother made the incredibly difficult decision to move him to respite care at a hospice facility, which was to be for a one-week stay. This temporary hiatus would provide Mom with the opportunity to rest, recuperate, and reevaluate his needs. While in respite care, my father's health failed to improve, and with a chilling realization, my mother knew that he would never come home again. He needed care, but not what she was able to provide. From respite care, my father was transferred to his final home, a group home. There, he was under weekly hospice supervision. My father's physicians seemed uncertain as to the time he had left. Nobody was able to provide the family with anything definitive about the timeline of his prognosis. In the past, when he had major health bouts with lung cancer, prostate cancer, and Burkett's lymphoma, he had defied the odds. I sensed that this time would be different. That was the weight of the universe I carried with me daily.

I have always paid close attention to my father's appearance and appreciated his essence. But on this day, at his bedside, I see in acute detail all the parts of him I'm desperately trying to memorize while time permits.

I see my father in the very parts that make him whole. His strong hands. His silky silver strands of well-placed hair (even in his deteriorated state). His silver bracelet, which never leaves his wrist, a shiny expression of his solidity and strength, now dangling loosely around his diminished wrist. I feel deeply saddened to see so much negative space around this once powerful symbol of his strength and self-assurance.

I smile as I remember the flex of his eyebrows or the upward turn of his smile, or how powerless I am to control the flutter of joy in my stomach just being with him.

Across the room, the analog clock is pulling me from my trance, flipping its numbers with each passing minute. Watch, wait, stare. I continue observing my dad, as time stampedes forward like a herd of elephants, fierce and unrelenting.

I've been seated by my father for what seems like an eternity, but only moments have passed. As I sit bearing witness to the hollowing of my father, I feel like I'm in a hospice time-transport machine. Entranced in memories, then startled to the present by surrounding noises. Back and forth I go. I remember a hug, a lunch with my father and then without warning, his caregiver breezes through the doorway to dispense his medication and awaken me from my saddened revelry. Where is the essence of my father? It's not within the body of the person I gaze upon, the person I've known my entire life. I hold his hand with such desperation to breathe even a glimmer of life into my father, to have a spark of connection for just one moment more. One more exchange, one more return squeeze from his warm, safe hands.

The hospice time machine entails having one foot in the unthinkable deep end of loss. Loss in their leaving. Loss in your losing them and loss of a love that slips through your fingers like sand. Like a balancing act, the other foot teeters through shared moments, remembrances of what was, to somehow buffer the pain of what will be. A bittersweet distraction. Anyone who has ever shared time and space with a loved one who's health is failing and whose life is passing, understands the desperate need to drink in every moment while feeling the cold, steely reality of death's imminence. Experiencing impending loss of a loved one is universal. We understand it, and yet, when the transformation from life to death is upon us, its cloak is paralyzing.

I return my gaze to my father's bushy black-and-gray peppered eyebrows, their warm expressiveness dramatically stilled. Off I drift to a place in time when their slight lift and fall would become the precursor to a joke, funny story, or fond memory. My father loved to tell a "good story." His stories will forever be emblazoned in the legacy of his family. "I was a medic in the Navy," he'd tell the family. Fascinated, wanting to hear more, I'd ask, "But you're not a doctor, Dad. What kinds of things did you have to do?" He would chuckle and continue, "Well, Deena, they train you. I did basic triage, and once in a while I'd have to give a guy an antibiotic shot in his butt." It made me laugh, thinking about him doing that, and even better, it made him laugh telling us.

I'm catapulted to one of my favorite Dad stories that he often told through tears of barely contained laughter. "You know your grandfather. You know what a stickler he was . . . He and Grandma knew the neighbor lady, Esther Mishkin. Esther would stop in once in a while and visit. One day, Esther stopped over and headed for the plastic-covered davenport and with a flip of her skirt sat down. She was wearing nothing underneath her skirt. Your grandfather was horrified and told me later, "Jesus, Sonny, her ass is stuck on the plastic. How do we get her out of here! Don't ever let her back in the house!"

Dad had a way of sharing a story that made people and things come to life. What follows is a story about him and about us.

Silver Boxes and
Shaving Cream

"Deena, please close the window blinds and make sure the bottoms are even before you walk away."

"Joan, see that, there's dust on the top of that bookshelf. Somebody needs to get that."

"Kids, please take your shoes off the couch."

I believe my father's persnickety ways were a direct result of his father's rigid ways. "Sonny, that's not right. That doesn't belong there." "Sonny, that's not how you do that. You're doing it wrong." Dad would recount to me when I was older that his father pointed out every imperfection and demanded it's opposite. It was imperative my father was on time, well-turned out, not idle, and always minding his father while working at the family store. At home, his father demanded everything was done "right," which meant *his* way.

In our world, the same commandments applied. Dad's expectations were equally as stringent. Therefore, my young mind assumed that my father meant business in whatever he did, including the possessions he kept.

The things he held close to his vest were that much more important because of who he was.

When you're young, your parents' room and accompanying cupboards, drawers, and cabinets make up an inner sanctum that's off limits. That's why when my father was getting ready for the day, I would often wriggle into his personal space to be a part of what he was doing. It was then I got to glimpse the shiny, engraved silver box with its purple velvet lining. Such an important box surely must have treasure inside. "Dad, what's inside the silver box?" I asked him one day.

"That's where I keep my pennies and change. Would you like to count it?" he replied. "If you count it, you may keep it."

Stop the earth's rotation right now. That's the best offer ever, I thought.

I left the bedroom with the tiny, surprisingly heavy, penny-laden silver box and headed carefully down the hall like I was carrying a pot of boiling water. Once in my room, I opened the delicate lid, tipped the box, and a cascade of bronze plummeted to the shag carpeting, with an occasional silver glint from an errant dime or nickel.

I counted the change, reported back to my father and returned the box. As it turned out, the coin acquisition was exciting, but even more magical was the purple, velvet-lined box. It was like being let into my dad's personal treasure collection. Anyone can have a box for pennies, but this was no ordinary box. My dad didn't have ordinary, run-of-the mill knick-knacks. If he had this box, it meant that there was something special about it. I never knew where the box came from, its history, or if it was an heirloom. All I knew was that it was special enough to be in his keep, and that made it special to me.

Many years later, when dad's health began to fail, I would stop over to the house for what I coined "pop-overs"—quick, impromptu visits. Often, it would be just my father and myself. One day, he asked me to follow him to his room. There, he opened a drawer and began sharing with me pieces of himself, pieces of his past, pieces that no longer made him whole. I knew, with a sad fluttering in my stomach, that those pieces would be the beginning of a collection that no matter how large would not bring him back. When I saw the silver box, I said, "I love that box. I used to count pennies from it. Remember?" My father nodded his affirmation and asked if I'd like to have it. My five-year-old self reemerged as I excitedly announced, "Oh, my gosh, yes. I would *love* to have that box!" Once again, I felt the magic bestowed upon me.

Brief magical moments seemed to frost my childhood, like the scented shaving cream my father used, which I can easily conjure in my souvenir of dad-memories. As children, sights, sounds, and smells leave impenetrable marks on our minds and hearts. Waxy crayons, warm Play-Doh, the sweet smell of aftershave lingering from a grandfather's hug, a buttery grilled cheese cut in triangular halves. The essence of these moments is emblazoned on our subconscious and through our senses. Even the scents from benign daily rituals can be emotionally stirring.

As a toddler, I would often saunter into my parents' bedroom and attached bathroom while my father was getting ready for work. He had important things to do to start his day, and shaving was at the top of the list. I'd sit atop the tub flanking his vanity and watched with rapt attention as his ritual began. First a shake, then the pop of the top of the can of shaving cream. Dad would load his palm with a large, foamy mound and begin patting his face, from his neck, to below his ears and even close to his nostrils. I watched every move. I was as amazed that he never managed to get any shaving cream up his nose. Completely covered, my father looked like he had a snowy beard. And then, the moment I loved. He would tap a dollop of cream on the tip of my nose.

I remember feeling enthralled that I smelled like my sweet dad in his important suit. Early in my marriage, I shared the impact of those moments with my husband, Sandy. To this day, if Sandy taps a dollop of shaving cream on my nose, the tears flow from a well so deep inside me, it defies words.

Rules My Father Lived By

"Jesus, did you sleep in that shirt. It's full of wrinkles.
You can't wear that!" we would hear often in our house. My dad was handsome and simply the best dressed guy we all knew. When my father wasn't adorned in his beloved Western gear (he loved anything having to do with horses and Western Wear), he was often seen sporting expensive belts with shiny buckles, jeans starched with leg creases sharp like sheet metal, and equally starched shirts, vests, and jackets, and buttery leather loafers. Over the years, I would learn from my father about pant hem length and the appropriate "break" as the pants hover above a shoe, vents, epaulettes, pocket squares, Windsor knots, and everything I needed to write a men's fashion essay.

When the family went somewhere important, my brother, sister, and I were given the autonomy to "get dressed nice" and select our outfits. One by one, like the Von Trapp family, we would then file in for inspection in front of my father whether he was seated in front of the television, or in the kitchen, or in front of an open pickle jar, where he could often be found. Wrinkled garments were completely unacceptable, and you would be immediately turned away. My father would not have his kids looking like "they just rolled out of bed and schlumpy." Hole-laden garments were a punishable offense.

My father's rules about how to dress were king. Footwear had its own inspection protocol. In the early 70s, when I was a toddler, white patent leather party shoes were all the rage and my favorite thing to wear. I can still smell the leather and hear the squeak as my shoes grazed against each other.

One morning, I readied myself for high-holiday services at temple. Proud as a peacock in my party dress, lace-trimmed socks, and white patent leather Mary Janes, surely I would pass inspection. I sauntered toward my father, chin in the air, defiant. There was no way I wouldn't pass muster. Front and center and *stop*. My father commented, "Deena, your shoes. They have black scuffs. What did you do?"

"What scuffs?" I replied with a huge smile.

"Deena, right there. Black scuffs. Look at your heels. You can't wear those like that! It's important to take care of your nice shoes." My father was obsessed with shoe care and deplored footwear blemishes, and more importantly, took pride in teaching us to care for what we had.

Make no mistake, I cared for my shoes. They were my favorites after all. Well, not according to my dad. If you didn't need eye protection, then your shoes weren't shiny enough. He was dead serious, and I was still laughing (not a good combination).

Determined to win my father's approval, I marched upstairs and put on my second favorite pair of shoes, white leather party loafers with criss-cross straps. *Boom, boom, boom* down the stairs and back in front of Dad. "OK, I'm done. I fixed my shoes."

"Deena, those are scuffed too. Are you dragging your feet like an ape? I've had the same shoes for years and have never had scuffs like that!" he exclaimed.

Completely undaunted, I blurted out, "OK, where's the shoe polish, I'll fix them." With that, he provided me the location of his prized shoe-shine kit.

Quick like lightning, off I went to make things right. I laid thick chalky streaks of white Kiwi polish on my shoes. When I finished my touch-up, the shoes looked as if they had been dipped in a vat of powdered sugar.

I returned tight-lipped and resolute in front of my father. (I confess, I tended to do things quickly and with less care than I should.) "Dad, I used your polish and put your kit back. Are my shoes OK now?"

Between chortles, he began, "Deena, you have to use a brush after the polish to shine them. It looks like you walked in chalk." Off I went again to brush out the caked on Kiwi polish.

Eventually, I got my shoes to shine and my father's nod of approval. I would learn to use a shoe-shine brush by watching my father—as he whisked the brush rhythmically against his boots and shoes—left right, left right—each week. Like film developing in a dark room, the shoes became brighter with each brisk pass of the brush. My father's shoe ritual was another opportunity to be in his company, a sliver of light into who this man was.

I learned about a person for whom grooming was ever important in his daily life. My father's generation knew the value of things and placed importance on taking care of what you have, rather than always replacing it with something new. As the years passed, we shared the love of a good garment, leather belt, snappy jacket, a fabulous pair of loafers, or a great mark-down at his favorite department store. Each time he shared with me, I knew I was being let in and took every opportunity to appreciate his words, his teachings, and him.

By the way, my mother did not escape my father's fashion rules of engagement. "Only hookers wear hoops!" my father declared. My mother was always well-dressed and accessorized. In the mid-70s, when hoop earrings were all the rage, she was thrilled to own her own her first pair. My father was horrified at the sight of her wearing them and demanded she remove the hoops from her ears. He had assigned negative connotations to the mid-sized gold circles, citing how cheap and tasteless they appeared. This was a horrifying and defining moment for my mother in her independence as a woman and fashionista. "You don't like them, then leave. I'm wearing hoops!" she defiantly announced to him. Ironically, my mother could have been the poster child for Emily Post, all class and lots of style. Her hoop-earring stance paid off, and he never mentioned it again. My father grew up with stringent expectations of manicured toes and fingers (he hated feet so much that the more camouflaged they were, the more tolerable), and lipstick when leaving the house. Some of his preconceived notions were a sign of the times, and some were old tapes he had from his conservative upbringing. Always look polished before setting a foot out the door. Wear the right thing. Do the right thing. "Right" became my father's guidepost but didn't soften with the change in times until later in his life.

Car Rules and a Double Order of Fries Please

"What the hell is that rattle? What is rattling in my car?!" My father, like a vehicular ninja, could hear noises in a car that would be inaudible to a dog. He was a car guru, hyper focused on dusty dashboards, too-loud radios, and the perfect paint color. Besides his horses, he also had a love affair with his cars. His cars were pristine. Their interiors, on any given day, looked and smelled as if they had just rolled off the dealer showroom floor. Their exteriors always shone. My father took pride in his belongings: horses, cars, shoes, they were all very well cared for.

On road trips or family errands, Andrea, Michael, and I would sit in the back seat of my father's car. Due to my small size, I was always relegated to "the hump." The hump is an awful place. It's where your elbow accidentally grazes your brother to the right of you, who, by the way, is disgusted he's in such close proximity to you. Your knee grazes your sister, on the left, who is frustrated she's in the car with everyone period, never mind crammed in the back with her arguing siblings.

My father had very stringent car rules. There were draconian guidelines to keep his chariots fastidiously clean. Gum in particular was a no-no in Dad's car. Bubble blowing, smacking, cracking, loud chewing, or even the scent of gum were enough to incite my father's ire. The most critical issue with gum was its disposal. He was hyper-vigilantly concerned it would end up stuck to his supple leather seats or on the floor of the car. Nevertheless, we persisted with our stealth chewing, thinking it would go under the radar. My father, however, like an echolocation sensing bat through rain, thunder, hail, or loud radio, somehow knew when we were chewing gum.

One day, while taking a family drive, I was seated on my assigned hump, which was highly visible in the rearview mirror. Unbeknownst to me, my father looked on as my jaw feverishly worked the gum. "Deena, get rid of that gum," he ordered. "I better not find it on my seat." *Of course, he won't find it on his seat. I'll put it in the ashtray. I'm not stupid*, I thought with a private chuckle.

Dad's keen sensibilities heard the faint click of the metal ashtray. "Deena, take out whatever you just put in the ashtray, and it had better not be gum." Michael and Andrea now feared what would become of their gum. They went on chewing quietly. "Deena, is that gum still in my ashtray?" Dad interrogated. "What did I tell you? Get it out of there right now, put it in a piece of paper, and hold it until we get to a garbage can. Don't drop it on the floor or get it on my seats. If your hands are sticky from the gum, keep them in your lap and don't touch anything." I did as I was told, all the while smiling smugly that I had somehow managed to chew my gum, get found out, and the earth didn't stop its rotation.

My young mind found humor in the intensity regarding my father's car and anything that took place within its confines. Then again, the more serious my father got, the funnier I thought he was. It's not that I provoked my father; I just didn't take some of his rules as seriously as my brother and sister did. I knew potential consequences wouldn't be earth-shattering, and so I was respectful of his rules, while putting a slight bend in them. Wide-eyed and towing the line, Andrea and Michael did what they were told. I did as well but felt a total lack of fear or concern at what would happen if the rules were not adhered to exactly. Dad's temper always blew over, at least for me. Dad was always stricter with Andrea and Michael. For me, somehow rules didn't apply. But for them, they were older and "should know better." I knew that once I got an inch from his nose, opened my eyes wide as an owl, and professed my love, his anger would melt away like hot wax cascading down a lit candle. After multiple attempts at car-related gum and food infraction attempts, the three of us minded the rules of our dad's car; his car behavior declarations would stay with us throughout the years like a Buddhist chant. Of course, it's completely ironic that cigarette smoking was en vogue and although somehow gum disposal was a heinous offense, sealing your three children in the back seat of a closed moving vehicle while billows of nicotine smoke barreled into their lungs was OK.

My father first asked me to accompany him to the car wash when I was around ten years old. Car wash day was important to my father, as he loved the sun glinting off the hood of his dirt-free car. The best part of the car wash was watching it go through the scary, loud machines. "See Deena, there it is, that's my car, it will be next," my father would say as we peered through the viewing window inside the station. Anticipation and excitement coursed through my veins. Silently, my father watched with intensity and focus, ensuring everything went smoothly. Out the other side, his beaming prize came, and off we would dash to retrieve his clean car. "C'mon Deena, it's ready. Let's go get in the car. Be very careful with your shoes. I just had it cleaned. Please don't put them on the seats." It was a ritual, the same each time and equally as exciting every time. Car wash day was important. It was typically Dad's day off on the weekend, and he had a more leisurely pace about his demeanor. I did not take his invitation lightly. My body tingled with joy. And, as if that wasn't enough, he asked, "Would you like to go to McDonald's afterward?"

My head nearly jettisoned off my shoulders, "Yes!" What a grand day: Dad all to myself, a car wash, and now French fries at my favorite place.

Sitting in McDonald's munching on my French fries, I said to him, "I can't wait to grow up, so I can drive."

"Why's that?" my dad asked.

"Because when I can drive, I'm going to McDonald's every day and getting two of everything!" We laughed at the irony that I barely finished anything I ate. Dad knew that two French fry orders was clearly potato in the sky thinking but went along with my fantasy nevertheless. I left McDonald's with a full belly and a feeling that I was somebody important that my father wanted to spend time with. Most kids crave one-on-one time with their parents, where their time spent is not about being parented, but doing something fun, maybe out of the ordinary routine of daily life.

As an adult, I've rarely been back to McDonald's, but a double French fry order has become my personal mantra for being able to accomplish whatever I set my mind to. My memories are not so much of the French fries and tasty burger, but of my father allowing my emotional spirit to take flight to fantastical places. Driving a car became symbolic of an older, independent me, confident, competent, and free as a bird. My father had a way of championing anything I desired. A seemingly mundane outing generated an extraordinary memory for me. These were the gifts my father gave me, sometimes in his utter silence and presence alone, where he may not even have known his impact.

The Revolving Caregiver

"I don't need anyone to *watch* me, Joan. Go do what you need to do. I'll be fine. I'm just going to watch the news and sleep anyway. What, are you going to pay someone to watch me sleep? Give me a break!" my father grumbled to my mother on multiple occasions. Even though my father felt he did not need care, his balance lacked stability, and he was weak. My mother wanted to know he was safe if she had to leave the house for a doctor's appointment or to pick up a prescription. This was a job for a caregiver.

Caregivers are selfless people who provide much needed physical and emotional care for those who are infirm due to a variety of causes. Trying to assist my ill father in the comfort of his own home, my mother worked feverishly to find the perfect caregiver for him. Dozens of phone calls, internet research, and unpleasant conversations with my father ensued. My father's health was a necessary but taboo topic, which made arranging care for him challenging. Frustrated and angered by the choices he was forced to make, he was unwilling to fully participate in the selection of his care, other than where complaints were concerned.

After several weeks, my mother identified a handful of caregiving agencies that would come to the house to do an initial intake, often bringing with them a caregiver designated for my father. It was like the ultimate nanny search.

Unwittingly, these angel spirits were crossing the threshold of arbitrary scrutiny. My father at heart never meant ill will, but his emotions were running high and his intolerance tank was on empty. Seemingly, only the thick-skinned would survive the litany of insults, put downs, and slander my father could dish out, although none did. When people are frustrated, they tend to lash out at the perpetrator. My father, however, would save up his complaints and then air them with my mother. So, while the caregivers who came to the house were never privy to his upset, my mother had to deal with a maelstrom of his criticisms.

Most of the caregivers passed muster with my mom. After the first caregiver interview, with a smile in her eyes, my mom asked my father to share his thoughts. "Jesus, she had sandals on. Her feet were dirty. I don't want to have to look at her toes and feet all day. Christ, don't they teach them how to dress?!" my father snarled.

OK, caregiver number one. Thank you for coming, but it looks like things won't work out.

Day after day, like a revolving door, these poor souls came and went. The next caregiver was petite and spoke Spanish. "I couldn't understand a goddamn thing she said!" my father groused. "And if I fall, she's going to pick me up? She couldn't lift a damn gallon of water. How do they hire these people, for god's sake!"

OK, caregiver number two. Thank you for coming, but it looks like things won't work out.

My mother was down to one final option, but my father pronounced, "She didn't say a freaking thing. What, are you paying her to sit in another room and read? What the hell kind of help is that? That's it. We are not doing this. I don't want any caregivers taking care of me." Like an electric current, the notion that my mother would have to continue being his caregiver, providing medical care she was untrained for, struck home. Since my mother wasn't a nurse or hospice nurse, she was unskilled at providing what my father needed.

My father brandished his complaints like a flimsy, foil sword. They really held no weight, but in the long run, my mother knew that if my father didn't have a good rapport with a caregiver, life would be a living hell for her. Frankly, being party to his play-by-play highlights felt like a living hell.

Ultimately, my mother cared for him within the scope of her abilities, until she no longer could provide him with the care he required. Her efforts were not without recourse. My father's nocturnal waking, transfers to and from the couch, bed and bathroom, doctor's appointments, and medication wore her out, both physically and emotionally. Simply stated, she was completely exhausted, while concurrently caring for the house, monthly bills, and managing the life they still had. So many people when caring for a loved one lose themselves in their fight to simply keep them alive. She devoted herself to holding him up at the expense of losing the pieces and parts that comprised her life: weekly Maj Jong games, lunches with friends, hair appointments, and even sleeping through the night. It was her joy to care for him always, even at the expense of herself.

The Coffee Klatch Kvetch

"That's the last time I'm getting a muffin from Panera.
It made me so sick. Deena, don't ever buy their muffins; they're under-cooked. That's what messed up my stomach!" my father explained when I called.

"Dad, so are you going to meet the guys someplace else then?" I asked.

"No, we always meet at Panera. It's good there!" he said. "I'll have the soup this time."

My father, although an inherently irritable person by nature, was happiest when distracted from his irritability by riding horses, spending time with the family, and lunching with his good friends. My dad loved going out to lunch. Mostly, he loved having lunch with his favorite buddies at the local grocery store coffee enclave, intermittently switching their gathering spot locations. My father had a knack for endearing himself to baristas to the point where they would have his donuts waiting for him at the counter or even hand-delivered where he sat.

Dad would tell me and the family about these lunches with his buddies. It was a love-hate relationship; he truly did love his friends, but he could easily become intolerant of them (or anyone for that matter).

"Dad, why do you eat with these guys if you get frustrated talking with them," I asked him one day.

"I don't know, Deena. I mean, some of them are OK, but Jesus, I don't know why I keep going honestly." This was my dad complaining about things he loved. He continued, "This one talks politics out of his ass, this one doesn't know his ass from his cellphone, and this one is just an asshole who argues!" Basically, his friends were apparently annoying yet endearing asses because this continued for years. He loved being with his gang despite his ongoing protestations. The sicker he got, the less tolerant he unintentionally became. His friends were loyal, kind, and understood that his health was rapidly unraveling before their eyes. Dad appreciated their constant support and was forever grateful in later months when they would pay him a visit at his group home. He truly did adore his friends. Like family though, the more you love 'em, the more you complain about them.

I would make it a point to pop over to his testosterone-filled coffee klatchs every now and then. When I'd kiss Dad hello, he'd pull me in tight and whisper, "Don't kiss that one. He has a cold." Ever my protector, he had certain friends he felt were not worthy of my affections.

As Dad's health declined, his ability to meet his friends for lunch dwindled and ultimately ceased. As much aggravation as he said it caused him, he dearly counted on those gatherings and religiously attended them, even to the point where he would go by himself and await anyone who would show up.

One day I found him sitting alone with a cup and a crumb-filled napkin where a pastry had been. His wallet and silver horse keychain were on the table.

"Where are the guys?" I asked.

"I don't know, Dee. This one said he would be here. Who knows? I'm going to wait a bit longer and take off. How's business? What's new?" And just like that, it didn't matter that his friends weren't there. It was a slice of heaven in my day when I could sit with my dad and kibbitz.

Once Dad was confined to his home and unable to meet his friends, I let him know I was available any time, either to drop off food or pop over for lunch. It was common for the phone to ring at my office around 11:30 am, and Dad would be on the other end of the line, asking, "What are you doing?"

"I'm working, Dad. What's happening? How are you doing today?" I knew he was calling for lunch of some kind. His taste for food and the ability to eat it changed daily. "You hungry? You craving anything special?"

"I'm OK. Have you eaten yet?" he'd ask.

"No, I could pick something up and bring it to your house."

And just like that, I'd hear his voice perk up. "Are you sure it's not a hassle? Yeah, that sounds great. Let's see, what are you driving by?"

Truth be told, en route to my parents' house, there were not many food establishments, but I was willing to get him whatever he wanted, whatever he was able to eat, if only to put a smile on his face and some food in his belly. "How about Subway? Does that sound good?"

"Ooh, yeah. You know what? OK, you got a pen handy?" and he'd begin to rattle off enough ingredients to stock a pantry, which compiled his toasted Italian Subway sandwich.

When I got him set up with a glass of water and his sub, I felt like I was five years old hoping to pass shoe inspection.

My father unwrapped the crisp sandwich paper with surgical precision, ensuring it lay completely flat before he consumed any food. Things had to be orderly, even if it was just sandwich paper. After a lift of the bread and a long stare, he took his first bite. "Jesus, I can't eat this. It tastes like the salami was in the bottom of someone's shoes! They always screw up my sandwich!"

My stomach plummeted with momentary disappointment, but then came the understanding that my father was not in control of his taste buds or digestive system. Trying to make everything better, I cajoled, "I'm sure it's fine. Maybe you're just not having a taste for it today, you know?"

"No, Deena. They don't know what they're doing. They get these kids, and it tastes like shit. I can't eat this!"

Well, there was one thing I knew I could get into my father's stomach. "Hey Dad, how about a chocolate pudding?"

"Yeah, that sounds good." All was right again with the world as he consumed his toddler-sized Jell-O pudding. And, much like the meal started, my father folded, bundled, and assembled his trash as fastidiously as the opening of his shitty sandwich. His perfect clean-up heralded the end of his meal.

The crazy thing about my father's illness was that it was hard to parse out his normal complaints about things (which was mostly everything), and the fact that his body was not providing normal taste sensations or the ability to digest properly. No matter what, I continued to bring over whatever his heart desired and would happily sit through the Academy Award-winning faces and monologues just because I wanted him to feel good and loved being with him. He'd done it for me when I was sick. It was part of our dance; we always took care of each other.

Lunch wasn't the only meal that challenged my father's constitution. Dinner became a nightly ordeal not only for my father but my mother as well. She took such incredible care of him, ensuring that his every whim was met. Dinnertime was the most challenging of all, as my father was unable to anticipate what or if he would desire food. My mother would begin the ask around 4 pm: "Marc, do you know what you might have a taste for? I'll make it for you for dinner."

"Jesus, Joan, I don't know. I'm not hungry. Everything tastes dry. I'll eat what you're making. Just go ahead and cook what you planned to eat for yourself," he'd reply. My parents performed this nightly food duet for months on end.

Mom: "Marc, what would you like for dinner?"

Dad: "Jesus, Joan, I don't know."

Mom: "Marc, I'm happy to make whatever you want. I just need to know so I can prepare or defrost something that you like."

Dad: "Don't go to any special trouble for me. I'll eat what you're eating. What are you eating?"

Mom: "I'm eating a salad with hard boiled eggs."

Dad: "I don't want a salad."

And then began the litany of pantry, freezer, and leftover options like roll call at a meeting:

Mom: "OK, Marc, I'll give you options, since you can't think of anything. How about scrambled eggs and toast?"

Dad: "Nah, that sounds terrible. What else?"

Mom: "Frozen spaghetti. I can defrost."

Dad: "Nah, I can't taste it. There's no seasoning."

Mom: "You want a baked potato with sour cream?"

Dad: "Yeah, OK, yeah, that sounds good. Thanks."

Despite all her planning and pantry prep, rare was the day that Mom could find something palatable to him. Simply stated, she needed help. Andrea and I came up with a plan.

"Mom, Andrea, and I have developed a service we call "Foober." It's "food uber" for Dad. Three or four times a week, she and I will take turns calling Dad to ask him what he would like from his favorite restaurants. This will give you a break a few nights a week. What do you think?" She loved it! Now, time to present the idea to Dad.

"Hi, Dad. So Andrea and I were thinking, you know, that it would help Mom a little if she had a few nights off from cooking, and we know you've been craving some of your favorite foods, so we created a service called "Foober." Anyway, several nights a week, a few hours before dinner, we'll call you to see what you're craving. Andrea and I will take turns delivering your dinner. What do you think?"

"So, like . . . what if I want chicken nuggets from Cane's?" he asked.

"Yup, Canes, Chompie's Deli, wherever and whatever you want!" I offered.

"OK, well, if your mom is OK with it, yeah, that works for me. So who will be delivering tomorrow? I want to put my order in!"

I felt strongly that any good service deserved a proper logo. With that, I set about crafting a custom design and t-shirts. Andrea and I created Animojis of ourselves that we used in the logo.

The best part of it all was that my father was having a blast. "Deena, I'm looking at other vendors. Your service is a little slow, and the French fries on the last delivery were cold." He'd smile, chuckle, and razz us (never mind, I had driven 20 minutes to and from the restaurant). When I asked him if there was anything else I could get him, he replied, "Yeah, new French fries." He began to anticipate his meal deliveries of Subway sandwiches, chicken nuggets, hamburgers, and even homemade entrees that Andrea and I prepared. He kept a notepad to jot down his food delivery options.

Our Foober service lasted for a month or two, not because of Dad's threat to hire a new food delivery service vendor, but rather his eating became an even greater challenge, something our cute t-shirts and smiles couldn't improve. In reality, Foober ended up delivering not only my father's dinner, but some of our father back to us.

Clothes Captioned

"What a putz. That guy's pants are two inches too short. When he crosses his legs, they look like knickers. What's with the black socks? Probably just finished mowing the lawn. Asshole!"

"Daaaad!"

"What, Deena? It's true!"

My father noticed every detail of people's appearances. Schlumpy shirts, banged up shoes, tattoos, piercings, or hair color. "Don't these people look in a mirror before they go out?" he'd often declare. He was a self-proclaimed connoisseur (he *did* have fabulous taste and style). Clothing and accompanying accessories were king. My father was not only a good dresser, he was also well-accessorized with his pocket squares, blazers, interchangeable belt buckles, and coveted black sunglasses.

At one point, he even had a professional headshot taken for a brief stint as a model for an industrial catalog and then a stunt photo of Columbo, who he was often mistaken for in his younger years.

His black sunglasses were not only a fashion statement, but a tool to avoid eye contact and a necessity at funerals, graduations, and other emotion-filled events. Even at restaurants, where nothing gut-wrenching but dinner ordering was happening. Historically a private person, my father was never one to be seen in an emotional state or crying for that matter. He emoted behind the safety of his cool shades. In fact, he ate dinner in his cool black shades. When my father checked in to his group home, he had with him his black eyewear, temples folded neatly, placed on his bedside table, even though he would never don them again. At a time when emotion increasingly bubbled over, he allowed me to witness his feelings without his protective black eye shields.

As Dad lost weight due to his illness, his desire to look like the best-dressed guy I knew never matched his decline. We spent a lot of time shopping together throughout the years. I loved doing pop-overs, during which he'd excitedly share his latest acquisitions. We both loved clothing and accessories—leather belts, shoes, and jackets with multiple pockets. My father loved jackets especially and had a different one for every season and occasion.

Because of his extreme weight loss, he felt cold most of the time. He told me he was looking for a lightweight jacket, with no collar, and a t-shirt waistband—something comfortable *and* fashionable. Something he could wear at home, feel good, and of course look worthy of receiving a visitor. As usual, he was very specific about his requirements. He may have been sick, but he would not be caught looking like a "shlepper." Out I went to search high and low for this holy grail of jackets. Tenacious in my efforts, I purchased and returned multiple jackets that did not pass muster.

One day, I proudly landed in my parent's family room to find my father seated in his regular, corner-most spot on the couch. "Dad, I found you the best jacket. You're gonna love it!" (For the record, you must know that "the best" was a term I used for many things, so naturally, my father was already fairly skeptical.)

Out of a shopping bag I lofted a black, racing style jacket, with white stripes down each sleeve. I waited for approval. Dad inspected the jacket from side to side, top to bottom, and checked the number of pockets. The heavy silence while he performed his inspection was deafening.

He wobbled his way to standing to try it on. Passing the initial phase of his piqued interest was gratifying enough for me. He put the jacket on, ambled unstably to the mirror, and declared, "We have a winner!" Fireworks of joy went off in my head.

A few days later, Dad asked, "Deena, where did you get that black jacket?"

"Ross (Dress for Less)."

The inquisition continued. "Deena, what department did the jacket come from?"

"Why?" I asked.

"Because Deena, this is a woman's jacket and the zipper is on the wrong side. Where did it come from?"

"Well, it came from women's, but I figured it would be OK. Who looks at zippers? It fits."

"Deena,"—he always invoked my name in advance of a joke or lesson—"it matters to *me*. I'm not wearing a women's jacket. What section did it come from in the women's department?"

"Well, it kinda came from the girl's section." And there it was: the black jacket elephant in the room.

"Jesus Christ, Deena! Do me a favor and stop shopping for me! The sleeves are up to my wrists and the girl's section . . . really? Now I'm wearing little girls' clothes?"

He did have a point, I thought, but if he didn't want the jacket, I'd keep it for myself.

A few weeks later, I breezed into my parent's family room.

Dad asked, "Deena, is that my jacket you're wearing?"

"Well, yeah. It was only $10 dollars, and I kinda liked it, so I kept it."

With a smile, he said, "That's nice. So now we wear the same size clothes. I feel much better!"

Despite his appreciative gruffness at my shopping efforts, I couldn't seem to control my retail compulsion to outfit my father in whatever he needed to feel or look good. Ever self-conscious of his dwindling stature, my father hated looking schlumpy. His slight frame was no excuse for not looking well turned out, even when he was only visible from the waist up under his blankets. At least in his mind, these were the rules.

In the early days of his residence at the group home, my father would get dressed and ready for his day. An occasional friend or family member might visit, and naturally, he liked to look good for the nurses and caregivers.

For years, my father's go-to favorite garment was a white, terry-cloth, zip up cabana jacket. He wore it until it was threadbare, yellowed, and looked like an old kitchen towel. When he moved into his group home, he did not take it with him.

Instead, he took a beautiful, white Nautica hoodie jacket which I had purchased for him a month earlier, even though he loathed the hood on it.

"Deena, you know I love you and always appreciate when you try to help, but I hate hoodies. Don't ever buy me anything with a hood again," he told me when I gifted him his hoodie.

I must admit, although I found some humor in the absurdity of his distinct clothing preferences, I felt a little disappointed. Yet I remained tireless in my shopping efforts, despite his repeated rebuffs of my purchases for him.

For someone who complained how awful something was, his actions surely were confusing. During one of my visits, I made the grievous error of pointing this out. "Dad, I notice you're still wearing the hoodie I got you. You like it now?"

"No, Deena, I hate hoods. I just don't have anything else."

I felt a bit of air and laughter escape from my ego balloon. Even though I loved my father's directness, it sometimes made me wince.

Most days, it was this very same hoodie that my father wore at the group home as he sat in bed with his hair neatly combed and his face freshly shaven. I saw a softened resolve, a withered spirit, and a garment that swaddled his frail frame. I was comforted by his regular use of the jacket, as it obviously was a source of comfort for him.

Doppelganger Den

"What are the shitty couches doing here!" My father growled to my mother and me moments after his arrival at the group home. My mother and I never anticipated such a response when she and I conspired in the transferring of his belongings from home to his new bedroom. Prior to Dad's transition to the group home, my mother and I predicted what moving into his new space would feel like for him. The group home itself was a magnificent, luxury-style property, surrounded by beautiful palms, cacti, and xeriscaping at the entrance. My father's room sat at the rear of the property, providing him with a private patio and beautiful courtyard view. The patio not only offered my father a window to the world of light and nature, but we would come to learn, it was also a blessing for safe connection during the pandemic.

I knew at the very moment I saw my father in his new space that he would never be coming home again. It's a heart-numbing reality when loved ones leave their dwelling of comfort, safety, and memories and enter a facility that will, for the remainder of their lives, be a mere stunt double. Never again will I see my father seated in his corner of the couch. There didn't need to be a dedicated placard or engraved brick for any family member or close family friend to know where my father's spot on the couch was. The concavity of the seat and back cushions were a shadow of his frame and a ghost of his past presence. I will never see him channel-surfing to find the news. Never again will I hear him say, "Hey, Dee, would you mind grabbing me a cold bottle of water?" Never again will I mark the cap in black Sharpie, with the letter M to indicate it was his, and never again would I switch this cap to a new bottle once he had drained the first. I was now permanently relieved of a duty I was unready to relinquish.

My father was in a temporary hospice facility under respite care for one week prior to the group home. As hospice prepared his transport to the group home, my mother and I scrambled to obtain a truck to relocate his couches, treasured gray leather recliner, cowboy décor, photos, and knickknacks, so that his new space would feel like a doppelganger of his coveted den.

After many machinations and the juggling of pick-ups and drop-offs, the "stage" was set. That's exactly what my father said it felt like—"a movie set." Seriously agitated at his belongings in this new space, he launched into a litany of conspiracy theories that this facility was really a front for a Romanian money laundering operation. "Look at this! You had to bring *my* furniture. If they were real, they would provide it for you. What a sham!" My mother and I tried to explain that we had them remove their furniture so we could bring in his. To this, my father replied with a swing of his hand, "Awww, bullshit!" My mom and I didn't know whether to laugh or cry, out of a sheer combination of emotional drain and physical fatigue. To my father, it was no laughing matter. For what Mom was paying, why couldn't they afford to furnish the space, he wondered. "My body may not be working," he argued, "but there's nothing wrong with my brain, and I'm telling you something is not right here. This is a racket, a hustle. They're taking your money and giving you shit. The people running around helping you are actors."

My father's rant went on for days. Mom, my sister, Andrea, and I sat and listened until he ran out of steam. Eventually, he came to terms with his new home and abandoned his conspiracy theories. We knew his rantings were borne of his utter lack of control over himself and his life as well as his decline in cognition due to the medications he was taking. For years, my mother had provided him with all his creature comforts, and in his estimation, there was nobody else on the planet who could do the same. Perhaps this was true, but there were many capable people in his new home who could provide him quality, nurturing care. Once he saw that his Ensure, pudding cups, and coveted Lay's potato chips were delivered to him upon his asking, his tune changed, and he settled in quite nicely, which was a source of comfort to the family. If he was good, then we were good.

More stark was the realization that my mother and father would never be a duo again in the same space. It was unfathomable to think they ceased to function as a unit, but rather as two people in separate worlds. Loving from afar would be the most painful exercise they'd participate in, in the history of their lives together. How many husbands and wives have performed this same dance? Bound by love, then marriage, and then by an unplanned separation in order to necessitate survival. Apart, but desperately working to remain together for as long as their fates will allow. My mother in the coming months would visit my father (while the pandemic allowed) and would speak with my father on the phone multiple times a day. They always remained connected.

Every day I visit my father without fail. Whether on lunch break from work, following errands, or at the start of a new day, my only goal is to see my father and let him know he is not alone, despite his change of residence. After all, wasn't home about the people and hearts who are with you? My connection and visits to him are simply an issue of proximity. If I can hand him a portion of his reins back and provide him some control and normalcy, then my heart will soar.

The quiet, residential neighborhood cleverly hid the fact that this was a group home. The circular driveway and tall front door shone beneath the Arizona sky. My father brought to this beautifully appointed place with its caring staff a broken-down body and spirit that required 24-hour care, care my mother was no longer able to safely provide after having tended to his needs for more than 20 years as he navigated a handful of cancer and heart-related issues. The move was a painful but necessary realization for both of them. My father felt helpless at the unwitting cruelty of his decline. Although in constant back and bone pain from his frailty, my father still waxed and waned with spark and the will to live. In a gradual yet sudden onset, his independence was leaching away. His new lifeline was a pendant "buzzer" tethered around his neck on a cord. The facility required the buzzer to summon help, whether it was for food or assistance with the bathroom. I felt humiliated that such a proud man now needed such a device. "I hate this friggin' thing!" he'd always say. It was a veritable anvil around his neck. *The veritable anvil pendant.*

I'm staring at my father as the news blares from his television. His once beloved pastime of watching the news is no longer a viable activity because of his profound hearing loss and lack of ability to focus for prolonged periods.

I watch my father fumble for the TV remote, which is the only task he can execute independently. After several moments, he successfully lowers the volume so we can visit.

When my father needs something—food, a beverage, blankets, or to register a complaint (which he did often at the beginning of his stay)—he presses a button on the pendant around his neck. My father despises this pendant.

"You know, for the money they're making here, you think they could afford something nicer than this plastic piece of shit," he tells me. I know he feels captive to it, but he also knows it's his lifeline.

I watch him fidgeting with the pendant as he ensures he knows where it is always. As the days and weeks pass, his vigilance wanes, and he's unable to locate it or even remember the protocol for using it. This wily disc seems to play hide and seek among rumpled sheets or beneath the folds of his white hoodie, which he wears daily.

At some point, my father loses his anger about the pendant and becomes agitated if he doesn't know where it is. He knows it's his portal to 24-hour care and occasional companionship to his solitary existence on the deserted island of his room.

I feel deeply saddened that somehow his most prized possession had morphed from a horse into a lousy lanyard and speaker button, but I'm grateful that his foggy cognition spares him the humiliation that would depress him severely.

With designated visiting hours and eventual visiting prohibited due to the pandemic, my family is grateful for the emergency pendant because it is Dad's lifeline to care in our absence. In a strange twist of fate, the little "piece of shit" ends up bringing everyone peace of mind.

My father's other lifeline is his cellphone. He can still manage a quick finger tap to call family and friends. Although his care team breezed in and out of his room daily, there was a sense of isolation when he was removed from the home he loved. Prior to the pandemic, in the early days of his residence at the group home, my father's beloved close friends would bring him milkshakes and lunch if he had an appetite to eat, and surround his bed with love, laughter, and distraction. When his friends weren't there in person, they called to say hello and let him know that although he no longer filled a seat at their weekly lunch table, he was with them daily in their thoughts.

Gabriel is the group homeowner. He has the kindest most patient soul, and after much pushback from my father, is a trusted ally for him and the family. Gabriel tirelessly and effortlessly is working for my father's trust, smiling while he happily acts on any culinary whim my father has, whether it's for a baked potato and sour cream, potato chips, or hotdogs. Gabriel will do anything for my father—move the bed, close the door, get more Boost or Gatorade, prepare whatever meals he craves, and allow the family snippets of COVID-19 safe visits.

Gabriel becomes our eyes when we are no longer allowed visitations due to the pandemic. He calls with updates and allows us to call at any hour, even humoring our desire to gather unimportant details of the day, which somehow makes us all feel a little bit closer to Dad.

Snap To

The institutional smell of bleach and the distant hushed voices from other patient rooms begin to pull me unexpectedly back to the hard chair beneath me and my father's unrelenting stillness. I stare intently at him, willing him to turn and look at me, one last time. Oh, how I would welcome hearing him tell me how loud the caregivers are, how noisy the kitchen is, and how terrible their hotdogs are. "How do you screw up a hotdog?" Dad would announce to the family.

My father's eyes remain open, staring upward, fixed. It seems as if he's focused on where he's headed. It's unsettling and hard to look at. I can't help feeling he's not ready to give in. Closing his eyes would mean his long, hard fight is over, and I feel he's holding on dearly to every moment, as me and my family remain alongside him.

My father's group home is lovely as is his care team. Each time I visit, something funny or memorable seems to happen. Like the afternoon the woman in the room next to Dad's started ranting wildly and loudly. My father is stewing as her shrill voice escalates. Finally, like a volcanic eruption, my father yells, "Put a fucking cork in it, you dumb ass! Jesus, can't someone get her to shut up? She's so goddamn loud. I don't need this shit!" In this moment, his crass outburst is funny, but I am profoundly saddened by the anger and helplessness at his lot.

This woman would be a constant source of aggravation for my father during his time there, along with caregivers whose accents he can't understand, who don't know how to tuck him in, dispense his medication, or do things the way he likes. Eventually, he will have them all trained to his liking and welcome the concierge services he will receive—including special visits to the store for Lay's Classic Potato Chips, which are hand delivered by the group homeowner, Gabriel. Whether it's a car dealership or a group home, my father is always finagling to get what he wants or needs. "Marc, you hungry today, what do you have a taste for?" Gabriel asks on any given day.

"You know, I'd love some potato chips. You going to the store? Would you mind? You don't need to make a special trip for me," my dad would softly counter.

"No, no, Marc, it's ok. I have to go anyway. What kind? I'll have them for you this afternoon!" And just like that, everyone is happy. Dad revels in the anticipation of his potato chip delivery, Gabriel, at his ability to assist my father and make him happy. In between Gabriel's many store runs, Andrea, Mom, and I drop off a deluge of snacks: peanut M&M's, pretzels, candy bars, and multiple Gatorade flavors which must be in small bottles. "Hey, Deena, tell your mom or sister, next time you stop in, would you mind picking me up some . . ." And whatever it is, within 24-hours, his wish is granted. We ultimately find out that whatever is left uneaten is sadly stashed by the caregivers in his bottom dresser drawer.

Freckles and Floaters

"Someone's freckles need counting. I'm not sure whose?!"
my father would declare. When I was growing up, my cheeks were speckled with freckles. On the top of my nose, they even congregated to form a more perfect freckle union. I hated them.

When you don't like something about yourself, but then see it through the eyes of someone who does, suddenly, it feels like the greatest thing ever. My father adored my freckles, so in my youthful mind, that meant they were more than OK. I became one with the tiny brown flecks and at peace with their permanent appearance on my face.

The thing I learned about freckles is, they're just spots until they have someone who loves them and loves to count them! Some of my fondest memories are of my father pleading for me to hop atop his lap so he could do this. Up I went without hesitation, and one by one, he ticked them off, "Let's see. One, two, oh, here's more, three, four . . ." Fireworks of joy exploded in my heart each and every time. He found lightness in my teeny facial specks, and I found lightness in his heart and soul. He was playful with me and my spirit. The place I always longed to be was in his lap, beneath his adoring gaze and tapping fingertips. At times when I was away from my father for sleepovers or camp, I would miss and wonder who would know how to count my freckles properly. At least where overnight camp was concerned, although he wasn't there to tally, he always sent me off with the fullest tank of love.

Freckles are not spots of pigmentation. They are there to be counted, affirmed, and loved. Every one of my freckles has been accounted for, loved, and appreciated. I can still feel his warm fingertip tapping each freckle like it was yesterday. I wonder if he ever knew how much this meant to me. Something about my freckles made me feel my father's pride for me, as every child yearns to make his or her parents proud, for small things and big. Good grades, well-executed chores, and good manners usually put children in their parents' good graces.

Even as a toddler, I somehow knew my father had a sweet spot for me. I thought I could do anything without fault. I learned, however, at that tender age that this was not quite the case. My father loved to recount the following pool pooping fiasco quite frequently at family gatherings.

Andrea, Michael, Mom, Dad and I piled into our wood paneled station wagon for a treasured outing to the Jewish Community Center pool. JCC pool outings were coveted and frequent. My parents' friends and their children convened at the pool on weekends as a respite from the work week. I can still smell the waft of salted fries from the snack bar and see the fluorescent orange safety stripes on the cement pool decking steps.

As soon as we got there, my brother and sister jumped in and out of the pool with their respective rafts, frolicking beneath the hot summer sun. I took no time to leap—as best as one can leap—into the kiddie pool, which was flanked by hypervigilant parents in what looked like circular poolside group therapy.

Even as an adult, I've never been one to stop the fun for bodily functions. My sister and I can shop for hours without having to relieve ourselves. It's mind over bladder. However, my father would tell you differently based on my one and only pool infraction. I honestly don't know when or even how what happened, but suddenly there was an onset of loud screaming, scurrying, and blasts from the lifeguard's whistle to evacuate the pool. This was followed by the lifeguard shouting repeatedly "Evacuate the pool!" through his megaphone.

As the chaos ensued, I was distracted by small, dark floating bobbers in the water. Plainly stated, I had pooped in the pool. Unabashedly I yelled to my father, "Dad! Dad! Hey, Dad! I just pooped in the pool!" It hadn't occurred to my three-year-old brain that my little cannonballs were the reason for the ensuing chaos.

My father had heard me for certain. He looked like he wanted to head for the next state. "Deena, quiet! Get out right now!"

"But Dad, I pooped in the pool," I kept declaring loudly.

Once I was out of the pool and wrapped in a towel, my father began, "Deena, did you poop in the pool?" (as if this needed to be asked).

"Yes, I had to go."

Embarrassed yet mildly amused, my father said, "Deena, when you need to go to the bathroom, you have to get out of the pool. You can't just poop in a pool. This is a public pool. Do you know why they cleared the pool of people? Because *you pooped.*"

He vaulted me into his arms and made a speedy exit with my siblings and mother in tow.

"Hey, I just pooped in the pool!" I blurted out proudly to the occupants of each chair we passed on our way out. My father couldn't get the hell out of there fast enough.

As we left, my father's head spun around like a barn owl in hopes that the friends we were there with were oblivious (as if that were possible!). Despite my dad's embarrassment, he never punished, shamed, or made me feel badly for this episode. In later years, how "Deena pooped in the pool" would become a favorite tale of his to tell and mine to hear. Dad would enjoy sharing my brown gaff at family dinners or with close family friends. Each time we heard the story, it was as funny as the first time.

Warm Fuzzies and Snacks in a Pickle

Deena,

Wish I could be with you to celebrate this your 40th year. I can't believe that so many years have passed since I first saw your little face looking at me through all that dark hair. I have enjoyed your "raising" of me and your wonderful wit which you have passed on to your daughter. You possess a warmth that permeates everyone and everything you encounter. Stay as you are, don't change and be happy for many more birthdays to come. "You light up my life."

I love you,
Dad.

There were many ways my father and I took care of each other throughout the years, whether it was a heartfelt note or letter, simple hug, a newspaper and coffee delivery to his desk, or him helping me with advice. Even grooming.

I have always had very long hair. My father loved my long hair. "You looked like a monkey when you were born. We weren't sure who your mother was," he liked to joke. Not only did my father love doting on his own hair, but he loved to comb and tend to mine. On school nights, I'd wash my hair. Up until high school, my father would say, "Bring me your comb; I'll brush the tangles out." Seated between his knees on the floor, I'd watch television as my father gently removed a nest of tangled strands from my hair. "OK, now hand me your brush." He'd run the brush through my hair for a smooth and a finishing touch.

Afterward I'd hop up, gather my hair supplies, give him a hug, and say, "Thanks, Dad!" My father took care of me, whether it was my hair or when I felt sick.

One morning in my childhood began with the usual bustle about the house, with my siblings getting ready for school, lunches packed, and shaving cream applied to my father's face. A yank of his tie, straightening of his collar, and a methodical combing of his coveted hair. Every strand in place like an attentive soldier. I didn't need to see this ritual to know it was happening.

I could smell my father's sweet-scented aftershave down the hall, from my bedroom, where I lay with a thermometer in my mouth (thankfully, the rectal thermometer had been thrown away!) and the best set up any kid could have. My mom had deftly tucked me in like a burrito. I had a glass of water with a straw, Jell-O, and comic books. I wanted for nothing except to feel better.

My father breezed through my doorway, crisp in his fresh gray suit, ready for his workday travels. The love in his eyes and the empathic warmth in his voice were enough to rival the tiny, pink tasty, St. Joseph's Baby aspirin, which I craved even when I wasn't sick.

While I slept on and off most of the day, my father called to check on me. Through my fevered haze, I could hear my mother providing status reports.

Upon his return home early in the evening, he again appeared in my doorway, his tie loosened from a long day's work, his shirt softened of its pertness, but his smile still warm. "How's my girl?"

"I'm OK, Dad. Still feel kind of yucky."

"I'm sorry, sweetie. Here's a little something to make you feel better." And just like that, this weary traveler, tired and ready for the couch, reached behind his suit jacket and presented me with a box of crayons and new coloring book.

My memory bubble holds an image of him standing in the door-frame of my bedroom with goodies in hand. As in all other moments between us, it was not the smell of the waxy coloring sticks or the news-print coloring pages that gave me joy, but that my father always found ways of letting me know that everything would be OK and that he would always be there. And he was, always. It seemed "being OK" would be a theme in our lives. To this day, when I don't feel well, I still see a halo of him leaning in my doorway and always feel just a little bit better.

The plastic drinking straw is another seemingly run-of-the-mill item that calls to mind love and care and warm fuzzies. When my siblings and I weren't feeling 100 percent, or had been to the dentist or orthodontist, straws appeared. The straw of choice in our house was the "bendy" kind, which allowed you to drink while laying down.

During my father's decline, straws became an integral tool to take in nutrients. When he became unable to digest solid food, my father's diet morphed into the Ensure, protein shake, and McDonald's vanilla milkshake meal plan.

One day, as I headed to the group home, I stopped to pick up a milkshake. When I entered his room, he immediately saw the frosty treat and sang out, "Ooh!" I handed it to him and then watched for several minutes while he struggled to tear the paper off the straw. Finally, he turned to me and implored my help with his eyes.

He took a few sips from the now semi thawed shake and settled in for our visit. Our roles had reversed, and now I was the one providing the nurturing and care. I felt my breath catch. My strong, horse-riding, joke-telling, fiercely independent father was now crippled by his motor skill attrition, weakness, and muscle loss.

We would later learn that my father's decline was due to Cachexia, a weakness and wasting away of muscle due to severe chronic illness. Despite beating the odds against multiple terminal diagnoses, the irony that his muscles were giving in did not go unnoticed.

For many weeks to come, I would continue to bring vanilla milkshakes for my father, but now I would present his shake with the straw already in place. I didn't want my father's infirmity to overshadow the enjoyment of his favorite beverage. There were so few moments of joy during those days he lived life from his bed, that anything I could do to make those moments better was a no brainer for me. My father and I leaned on each other. Time would change the nature of support and who was doing the supporting. We would take turns providing for each other, shouldering the weight of each other's happy and sad moments.

I never paid much heed to shoulders, except for my father's.

If I was seated next to my father, my head was on his shoulder. When, in later years, he took up residency in the corner-most part of his couch, I would still find a way to rest my head on his shoulder. I believe I was the only one in the family who took advantage of this angular place of love. Well into my 50s, I continued to roost wherever my father would have me.

My father's shoulders were not particularly worth mentioning; there was nothing excessively muscular or spectacular about them, but they could hold the weight of my heart and ease my day. Beneath my cheek, my father's shoulder bolstered feelings of calm and peace and immeasurable joy. The sweet smell of his waning aftershave made me think that everything would be OK and I was in the safest place in the world. When he cupped my face in his hand and looked down at me with so much love, I felt I would burst. The strength in my father's shoulders was who he was: rock solid, accepting, and always there.

As his health took a turn for the worse, my father's shoulder became a place for my hand to comfort *him*, to let *him* know everything would be OK. I may not have been able to provide the same assurances his shoulder had given me throughout the years, but I think it was enough for him that I was there with him. I'm certain he never knew how much it meant to me to rest my head on him. This seemingly banal gesture was the world to me. Since his passing, I long to sidle up next to his slight frame, lay my head on his shoulder, and breathe him in one last time.

For now, I simply imagine my dad in his blue, plaid, long sleeve shirt, crisp from the cleaners, seated in his spot on the couch, waiting for me to sit down beside him. In my heart, he'll be there waiting in perpetuity.

Associations of my father lurk past the corner of the couch. Before food became his nemesis, snacking was another thing we shared, particularly if we were watching television together. My father loved a good snack! "Deena, grab the Doritos!" "Hey, should we make some popcorn?"

I often found myself sidled up to my father at the tall kitchen counters (I was always petite, so everything was tall and unreachable). "Dad, what are you eating?" I'd ask.

"Oh, I'm just grabbing a snack. Would you like some? Here, you go!" And with lighthearted gladness, he'd lop off large hunks of Hebrew National Kosher beef salami and place them in front of me on a paper plate. "You like that? You like salami? That's my girl!" he'd proudly say. More fireworks of joy for me! "How 'bout a pickle?" My father was the ultimate pickle connoisseur. They had to have lots of garlic and be well brined. His favorites were Don Herman's kosher pickles. On occasion, my father would substitute sauerkraut for pickles. All we were missing was the lederhosen and a biergarten. As if we didn't have enough savory gastric snacks in front of us, my father presented a small, square, metal can with a key. "Ever eat a sardine?" he asked. I screwed up my face in total disgust. There was no way I was going to eat teeny fish crammed in a Band-Aid size box. Ewwwww! I watched my father carefully place the key in the proper position to begin unscrewing the teeny box. "OK, here ya go. Try it." I expected the worst, but the sardines were good! My father was pleased as punch. It's no great surprise that my father had constant gastrointestinal upset.

Thereafter, on any given day, the two of us could be found at the kitchen counter ingesting our favorite nibbles. Our snacks smelled like a sewage plant to anyone within a foot of us for sure, but we loved it!

Fish Hooks and Extension Cords

My father's disposition when I was growing up was like an orange. He had a thick skin, but there was such sweetness under the peel. Of course, these pulpy, sweet parts were not something generally visible to rest of the family. My father tended to reserve them for waitress flirting, examination of his coveted hair (he carefully doted on his locks), or hoisting a saddle on his beloved horse.

Strict to the core with my brother, sister and I, chores were at the top of his "do them right" list. The most pressing: the daily dinner clean-up. There was to be order amongst the ranks, as each of us was relegated specific duties.

"Andrea, oversee your brother and sister. Wash and dry the dishes. Michael, assist Deena with table clearing and floor sweeping. Deena, clear the table," my father chimed nightly.

These posts were to be memorized and performed without question. The nightly culmination of dinner played out with my father standing over his emptied dinner plate, declaring, "Kids, help your mother." In other words, this fell under the category of "effort" and therefore, my father would soon be on the couch, with TV remote in hand, watching the news. At one time, these archaic, quintessential male/female roles ruled most homes. Mom cooks, cleans and tends to the children, while father governs from his couch. In our house, the couch was indeed a throne my father ruled from often. From the couch, he'd add, "I don't want your mother doing anything. She worked hard making dinner." Ironically, he was willing to ensure she had help, just not from him. Basically, Mom was on board with our assigned jobs, so she and my father presented a unified front.

I did not like being assigned tasks, as I was unmotivated to do any household chores, and I didn't want to be harassed in the kitchen. A tad willful, I marched to the tune of my own drummer. Once the three of us accepted our delegated responsibilities from my father (which were pre-approved by my mother), I knew there would be hell to pay when I entered the kitchen with my brother and sister. Working hard to find a crumb to prove my task incomplete, Michael would check my designated work area and say, "Nope, not good enough. Do it again!" At my brother's snarled directions, I found myself sweeping and re-sweeping, wiping, and re-wiping, and occasionally, ingesting a dirty kitchen sponge shoved in my mouth. I think it's safe to say, "Hell's Kitchen" originated in my house!

"You're not Dad. You're just making me do it, just to mess with me!"

Our classic sibling rivalry drove my sister crazy. She knew if chaos was audible from the kitchen, she would catch my father's verbal wrath, as if it was her fault. This left her in a foul and menacing mood. I may have been the youngest, but I was smart enough to know when to get the hell out of the kitchen! And I was also the smartest to approach the source of potential concern: my father. If I distracted him, I got out of my chores. It was a win-win plan!

The natural course of action was to excuse myself to the bathroom, but instead I'd approach my father on the couch.

"Deena, aren't you supposed to be helping in the kitchen?" my father would inquire.

I'd wedge myself between my dad's knees, bug my eyes out, and say, "What?"

He'd look at me in complete disbelief at my unflappable gumption and then release a small chuckle.

Light shone through a crack in my father's veneer, I pressed on. "Well, ya know, cowboy, I don't much like to clean the dishes," I exclaimed, mimicking John Wayne with my underdeveloped vocal cords.

Another chuckle, this one louder. My father leaned left then right then left again to see past me blocking his view of the TV.

This time, I'd try Jimmy Stewart. "Ya see, ya see, I don't want to, see . . ." I spouted. In a muddle of parental rage and joy, my father began to laugh! And there it was. I had his gruffness in the palm of my hand like warm clay. By the time I finished my improv and nestled myself on his lap, with my head tucked under chin, he was completely disarmed.

Unbeknownst to me, my sister and brother looked on slack jawed from the doorway, "What are you doing? You're supposed to be helping us. I thought you went to the bathroom, you little brat!" shouted Andrea through gnashing teeth.

"Oh, do you still need help? I'll come in now," I replied. Well, we all knew the answer to that. My shenanigans had lasted long enough to endear my father and get me out of helping in the kitchen. My mother would sit on the opposite side of the couch on a telephone call with a friend, nap, or watch the news alongside my father. Once we completed our jobs, my mother would pop in for an occasional inspection, noting a less than effective cleaning job behind the kitchen faucet.

I was nonplussed by my father's ramrod disposition. Why were my sister and brother so afraid of him? (I would come to learn that I had a knack for getting in the face of intimidating personalities.) And my sister would tell me he just plain laughed at anything I did.

My father's sternness meant nothing to me. I found his grizzly gruffness funny, and his armadillo façade a welcome challenge. My childhood was replete with these types of encounters. During these moments, I fish-hooked his inner kid, and we played and laughed. This is how I defied the odds of any punishment or consequence. I don't remember having awareness of how my actions affected my siblings or how my relationship with my father affected them. I just knew I loved Andrea and Michael to the moon and back. No matter how angry they would become at me and my antics, I had nothing but pure, unconditional love for them. I was a loyalist and through thick and thin would always tolerate whatever they dealt, even if they would take out their resentment on me. No matter what, I've always been uber-attached to anyone I love.

When my parents dropped me off at college, it was a cryapalooza fest for me, Mom, Dad, and even my brother. As Michael and I matured, so did our relationship. I could always count on him, and there was never a time he didn't offer to help me whenever I was in need. I love my brother dearly and have historically put him on a pedestal. I've since lowered the height setting and now we are on equal footing.

College was only a few hours from home, and my father often had business near campus. Each time he would come to town, I would be blessed with a visit and outing with my dad. "Where do you want to go? Is there anything you need?" he'd ask me. We'd go to the mall, to the grocery store to fill my fridge, or out to dinner with his business colleagues for delicious and much needed nourishing meals. I loved when my father would visit my dorm room, sit at my desk, and I got to sit in his lap. Fireworks of joy never faded, even as I got older.

He'd ask about school, and although he was right in front of me, I missed him already. On one outing to the campus mall, we walked past a plush animal store. Dad and I were suckers for anything cute and stuffed. "See anything you like?" he asked. Within seconds I locked eyes with a white fluffy lion. Without hesitation, Dad headed to the register to pay for my new friend. I named him Marcello. Marcello stayed with me throughout college, and I still have him today.

After graduating and moving out of the house, I still longed to stay connected with my family. I would call my parents quite frequently, to the point where my father would ask, "Deena, didn't I just talk to you yesterday? Nothing new has happened since then. Did you call to hear me breathe? Everything's good. I'm good. Mom's good. OK, I'll talk to you soon." Ironically, that was all I needed, to hear his voice and yes, to hear him breathe.

My parents' friends as well as our extended family would inquire, "When is she going to cut the cord?" I made everyone starkly aware there would be no cord-cutting ceremony as I had an extension cord, and that would suffice wherever I was for however long I needed it to be there. When you love, it's a joy to be tethered in perpetuity.

Butterfly Sneakers and the Pandemic Hourglass

Like a well-oiled machine, my father's caregivers are popping in and out to check on him. His vitals, his hunger, his thirst, his position in bed.

I watch these healthcare phantoms float in and out of the room like butterflies, their sneakers squishing softly on the linoleum floor around the perimeter of my father's bed as they attend to his needs. The sad irony is, in their attempts to not disturb him, that's exactly what they are doing.

The longer my father stays in this group home, the less control he has over his life and health. Ultimately, his stay in this group home will span just shy of four months before he will pass, with only the first few weeks of allowable visitations prior to the pandemic quarantine. I have friends and work colleagues who share similar trying experiences. Mothers, fathers, and grandparents who are unable see family. Heartbreaking visits taking place through windows, with pressed hands on either side of the glass in a desperate attempt to have contact with isolated, sick, and dying family members. Ours is one story of a million being told during the COVID-19 pandemic.

I believe this is why blankets become my dad's penultimate source of control. You wouldn't think a blanket would be a big deal, but when your entire world is beneath the folds of one, suddenly you understand.

"I need a new blanket. This blanket is terrible," he tells the caregivers. After several proffered blanket options, my father finally receives one to his liking.

But it's not enough that it's an acceptable blanket; it also needs to be smoothed, flat-laying, and, for god's sake, cover his feet. "Christ, they come in to fix my blanket and leave my feet uncovered. They don't know what they're doing. Deena, would you please cover my feet? They're freezing, thanks honey." My father is angered and disgusted that the caregivers aren't noticing his toes peeking out from his hiked-up blankets.

In this group home, there are a handful of caregivers, each on different shifts throughout the day and evening. Overall, the family is satisfied with the quality of care, but there are a few caregivers who are consistently aggravating my father. My father summons assistance by pressing the assist button on his pendant. "Hi, listen, my pillow is screwed up. I need it behind my neck, and I can't fix it." After much shuffling, the caregiver repositions both my father and his pillows, much to his moaning and protestations. I then hear, "Jesus, you'd think someone would teach her how to stick a pillow behind someone's head for god's sake!" One caregiver repeatedly seems to do the opposite of what my father wants. A few of the caregivers have accents he is having a hard time understanding, particularly since he's opted out of using his hearing aids, as they are becoming increasingly more difficult for him to insert into his ears. Eventually all the caregivers are learning to navigate his quirky and demanding requests, and my father is finding acceptance, tolerance, and trust in them as well. In essence, my mother had taken such good care of him over the years, that it is taking a great deal of faith and patience for him to trust someone else is up to the task as competently.

Besides blankets, my father remains somewhat tuned in to bits and pieces of the news, especially about the COVID-19 pandemic. With the pandemic worsening by the day, my family embraces each visit we're allowed with my father while understanding that additional restrictions may be imposed at any moment.

As I sit by my father's hospice bed, in the quiet of his life limbo, I feel his bravery as he reconciles being OK with the ending he knows is near, and willing the pain and suffering to leave his body after such an exhausting fight. He's had enough and has let us know.

As my father's health is beginning its severe and final decline, he requires morphine for pain and comfort, yet never does he close his eyes while under the logy veil the medication induces. Instead, they remain in a fixed, vacant stare. In classic Dad style he doesn't want to miss anything as he wages this fight. In his final days, his only focal point seems someplace so far away only he has access.

I am beginning to see the pain removing itself from his previously grimaced brow, falling away with each passing tick of the clock. Hospice coins this phase "transitioning"—a subtle, yet frighteningly obvious onset of departure. How unbelievable it is that I can observe my father change so dramatically from moment to moment, and yet still be OK with it?

I brush a lock of hair from his forehead and hear him muster an almost inaudible groan, which translates to "Stop messing with my hair" (he never let anyone touch his hair, not even my mom unless she was cutting it). I loved this flicker of Dad still being Dad. It takes only moments for him to fade back into his stupor, but I'm grateful for that brief life spark, although I've aggravated him.

Because Dad and I are so close, I don't have the stomach to joke about his death even when he has teased in the past about what kind of food he wants at his shiva. "Jesus, don't have shitty, stale rugelach from a lousy bakery!" This is my kryptonite, yet here I am, witnessing my father dying in real time. How quickly we mature when life demands it. My father is always matter of fact and instilled in me that death, although difficult, is a part of life and that I'll have to deal with it. So now, I suppose if he's OK with it, I will learn to be so as well.

Swearing Horses and Mini Wonders

As far back as I can remember, in contrast to a variety of favorite lunch buddies throughout the years, my father's true best friends had hooves (he always loved his human buddies, but horses seemed to penetrate his soul in ways his friends or others in his life couldn't). My father loved anything associated with horses, Western movies, and the desert landscape of the southwest. A self-proclaimed Jewish Cowboy, my father not only looked the bad-ass part when atop his favorite steed, but he lived and breathed horses daily. While most husbands and wives would awaken to discussions at the breakfast table, on weekends, and some weekdays, my father was out the door once the sun hit the horizon. Once my father was retired and living in Arizona, his visits to the stable became almost daily. My mother basically thought of herself as a horse widow when, much to her chagrin, Duke, my father's horse, practically became his significant other. The family often wondered how, with so much time spent with his horse, did he have time to make any friends at all!

My father developed a brood of stable friends throughout his life. Most of them were horses, and the rest were women. My father's stable buddies included stable-hands and others boarding their horses at the same location. My father, always the gregarious flirt, loved to participate in group trail rides with his posse. My mother knew that his loyalties were always with her and that my father was by nature a tireless and harmless flirt.

If you were asked to accompany my father to the stable, you would be witness to his undeniable expertise at hoisting saddles, picking hooves, tightening girths, adjusting reins, and most importantly, schmoozing in the tack shop over a steamy cup of coffee in the cool morning air. My dad gained his equestrian knowledge through years of riding, watching, and listening to fellow horse enthusiasts and stable friends. As long as he was near hay, neighs, and whinnies, he was truly in his happy place.

In one of my favorite photos of him, he sits atop Bay Sabar, his beautiful Arabian. "Here you go, Deena. I autographed it for you," he said when he gave it to me. Life happened to my father when he was at the stable. He had been stepped on, concussed, launched from his saddle, and entangled in a variety of other horse-related accidents, but even so he developed longstanding friendships and simply loved to sit on the barn porch in the early hours of the morning, watching the horses as they were turned out in the ring. My father loved seeing white bursts of biting winter air stream from their nostrils. He loved the smell of leather, the crunch of gravel under hoof. He loved patting their muscular necks, stroking their shiny manes and gently rubbing their pink velvety muzzles. He moved through life at the stable with total commitment and grace. "Deena, want to see something funny? Come here. My horse loves Altoids!"

Throughout the years, my father would own a handful of horses. There was Sassy, Bae Sabar, and his favorite and last, Duke, a beautiful, buff Arabian. My father was smitten with Duke and became very involved in Duke's healthcare.

Dad loved to share his love of horses with his children, grand-children, sons-in-law, and daughter-in-law. He'd hoist his grandkids proudly on his horse, walk them around, and take photos. Each of his grandkids was either taken to a Western store for the purchase of a hat, belt or boots, or would receive them during the holidays. Dad's equine passion had permeated the entire family.

I have fond memories of rising early and accompanying my father to the stable. He taught me to brush and care for horses, clean stalls and saddle up. "Deena, clean up the stall. If you want to ride a horse, you have to be able to shovel horse poop!" Occasionally, Dad would ensure there was a gentle pony for me to brush, walk the ring with, and safely ride. I will always love our tandem rides on his tall, strong horse, with my arms wrapped tightly around his waist as the horse trotted down a snow-laden path. I felt safe, and Dad felt at home in the saddle.

On one occasion, my father invited my husband Sandy to the stable, and Sandy was happy to go. Dad took him in to Duke's stall and announced it was "Teeth and Sheath Day," which meant the vet would be inserting his arm elbow deep into Duke's rectum and cleaning the horse's penis, while my father ripped a million jokes, including asking Sandy if he'd like to assist. "Teeth and Sheath Day" became a running joke between them for many years. Following this zany "southbound" event, for my father's 75th birthday party, I roasted him, accompanied by a gangster-sounding, rubber horse puppet that said, "Da udder day, I'm in my stall, minding my road apples, when Marc comes in . . . I hear da snap a da latex glove on Marc's hand and my mane stood on end . . . what the hell?! Next thing I know, with Marc's help, Dr. Oz has got me singing like Ethel Merman as he rids me a roids da size a grapefruits!" For Sandy, it was a memorable testament to the humor and love he always felt when spending time with my dad.

Dad's feisty personality didn't stop just with family and dogs (over the years we had several). Apparently, he could be quite testy with his horses as well. He told me, Mom, and Andrea about the time an equine horse whisperer made a visit to the stable where my father boarded Duke. "The whisperer lady," as he called her, was ambling around the property when she happened on my father and Duke. She spoke with my father and spent time with Duke. After several minutes communing with his horse, the horse whisperer sat down and began questioning him.

"So, Marc, tell me, how do you get along with Duke?"

Already challishing from what he felt was clearly a stupid question, he replied, "What do you mean, how do I get along with Duke? He's a horse. I brush him, feed him, and ride him!"

The horse whisperer nodded but clearly wanted more detail. "Marc, do you ever get frustrated with Duke?"

"Of course," Dad quickly replied. "Sometimes I'm trying to put a saddle on him, and he won't stand still. You try holding up a fifty-pound saddle while your horse is screwing around."

"Marc, what do you do when Duke doesn't listen?"

"I take him out for coffee. What do you think I do? I either have to use the crop to get him to settle or . . . I don't know. Why?"

"Well, it seems you've been swearing at your horse."

"Jesus, the horse told you I'm swearing at him? Nice, the horse is telling on me now?!" Dad sputtered while nodding condescendingly at the horse whisperer.

"Well, Marc, Duke doesn't like it," she chastised. "It's upsetting him. If you treated him more nicely, he might be more cooperative for you." There and then my father's bullshit meter became unhinged from its springs, and that was the end of the conversation. When he recounted this to Mom, Andrea, and myself, we howled with laughter.

"Why are you laughing?" Dad asked, looking surprised. "So what. I swear at the horse. It's a *freaking* horse for Christ's sake. That's bullshit the horse told her I was swearing. Horse whisperer my ass!"

My father's irreverent essence seeped from his pores whenever he had dirt beneath his boots and reins laced through his fingers well into his late 70s, when heart issues prevented him from any further horse riding. Procedural and post-surgical pain never matched the emotional loss of giving up Duke as well as the utter freedom and joy horse life brought to his soul. It would take months for him to recover from his sadness and a loss bigger than he understood. Fortunately, he and my mother would find renewed love and companionship with their new dog, Lexi, who was always at my father's side. Although Lexi never replaced my father's horse, he adored Lexi, and they quickly became kindred spirits. Lexi drew out a gentle warmth in my father. Together they would sit quietly on the couch or spooned in sleep on the bed. Lexi never left my father's side. While in his group home, my mom brought Lexi to visit my father. The joy that passed between dog and man was indescribable. With quiet love, Lexi spun around and placed herself in a circular mound beneath my father's arm, an easy place to rest and get petted and an even easier place for my father to feel at home.

Several years later, through work and life connections, I would create a few different opportunities for my father to safely engage with horses. I longed to create moments of horse- filled joy for him, even if it was bittersweet and only brief. I desperately longed to scoop out his pain-filled spaces and fill them with peace.

As my father declined, his ability to drive and walk distances became challenged. He was frail in body, but he was still able to come to my house. I was continually looking for ways to lift his heart and make him feel joy, despite the scary reality of what he was facing. And I was particularly focused on "giving him a piece of his lost horse soul back," if only for brief time.

I was delivering art I had created for an equine therapy client. Knowing it had been a few years since my father had given Duke away, I thought he might like to join me to have a horse encounter. As these were therapy horses, they were gentle and accustomed to people with all sorts of conditions and limitations.

My father happily agreed, and we drove to the ranch. Dressed in his classic blue and white plaid shirt, jeans, cowboy belt buckle, and hat, he looked like he was "back in the saddle" again.

Once we arrived, my client offered to bring out a horse for my father to brush as he was unable to walk to where the horses were located. It was beyond touching to see him quietly stroke the horse's side with the brush. He performed down strokes over and over again while he rubbed the horse's ears and cooed quietly to his snorting new friend.

My father had been reticent about seeing a horse again, but he trusted me and felt safe to allow me to orchestrate this reunion. The tranquility and wholeness my father experienced in that moment overwhelmed and saddened me. I stood by quietly, snapped a few photographs, and took in the sight of my father feeling serenity for a moment. One of my favorite photos from that special day was the two of us sitting side by side on a bench, sporting our boots.

I assumed this would be his final horse encounter, until he started telling us about a commercial he'd seen. Unexpectedly, my next opportunity arose when I learned of a miniature horse named Gentry.

My father watched a great deal of television. He'd love to recount commercials that he thought were hysterically funny. One such commercial involved a miniature horse named Anthony that lived in an apartment and would "fetch" things his owner needed. Dad liked to quote the commercial actor asking his horse to bring him his laptop ("Anthony, the computer").

My father had learned to live with the hole that was previously filled by his horse Duke and all that encompassed his horse life. As his health worsened, I wanted so badly to give him some of what he had lost. I could not give him the ability to ride horses again, but perhaps fill the emptiness and loss in some other way.

I believe there are no coincidences in life and, as such, it was serendipity that through my husband's Facebook page and a mutual friend, we happened upon a woman named Sandra and her miniature horse, Gentry.

The heavens opened up, and my heart filled with light. I knew at that moment that Gentry would be coming to my house. As Dad's ability to ambulate safely declined, coming to our house was one of the few outings he could still comfortably do.

As a surprise to for my father, I arranged for Sandra to bring Gentry, a beautiful, black-and-white miniature horse. The family knew of my plans and helped me orchestrate logistics of having all of us present and waiting on our back patio. Seated on our patio on a cool, October afternoon, my family visited as usual, awaiting the arrival of Sandra and Gentry. My father was seated in the swivel chair where we had suggested he sit. Little did he knew that he was about to have his own version of an "Anthony, the computer" moment.

I met Sandra in front of my house, and together we led Gentry around back toward the patio. "Dad, there's someone here to see you," I gently announced. As my father slowly swiveled in his chair, he was met with the vision of a beautiful little horse clip clopping over to him.

Time stopped. In that encapsulated moment, Dad was Dad. He was not sick Dad. He was not dying Dad. He was not infirm Dad. He was Dad with a horse. He fed Gentry carrots, rubbed the soft pink of Gentry's muzzle, tickled his nose, rubbed his ears, and asked Sandra questions about herself and the horse. He even taught Gentry a trick, rewarding him with baby carrots.

Two hours later, Sandra and Gentry left for home. Dad had few words and was visibly tired, as his stamina often dwindled easily. During her visit, Sandra had presented my father with a plush "mini-Gentry" horse, which my dad adored and kept under his wing during Gentry's visit. "Thank you, Deena. That was wonderful," he said quietly. It was one of those moments where no words were necessary. Watching my father in a horse-filled bubble of time was incredibly fulfilling. When my father was speechless, his wordlessness spoke volumes. Today was one of those days.

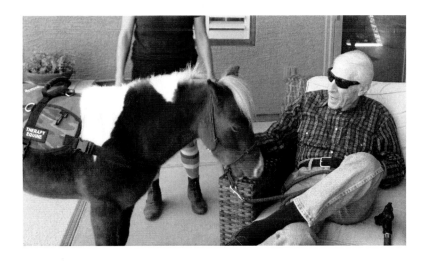

For a brief afternoon, my father's imminent terminal reality was eclipsed, and moments of his prior normalcy were had. He was able to feel coarse hair beneath his fingertips, and the calm, confident cowboy we all missed returned for a while.

Sugar Cubes and Bad Donuts

My father owned a manufacturer's rep business, called "Key Marketing," through which he represented products from manufacturers and sold them to stores. He was very successful, well-known, and highly respected in his industry. He had his own office, secretary, typewriters, and snacks (as a kid, I registered my father's work world via the snacks and samples at his office). The snack area at my father's office made quite the impression on me as a child, and so it sounded like a perfectly exciting place to go.

During summer break from school when I was around age ten, Dad asked me if I'd like to come to work with him and then have lunch. Without hesitation, I blurted out a resounding, "Yes! When?"

We made the arrangements, and I'm certain in my exuberance, that I was probably dressed and ready two days prior. Wanting to make my father proud, I donned what I knew would be an acceptable outfit. My father always dressed the part for work: on trend blazer, tie, slacks, and a fabulous pair of loafers. Now, with my shiny, clean face, and tasteful outfit, I felt fresh and ready to show my dad I was a hard worker.

A flip of the switch and the office was suddenly illuminated. Here was the place he spent his days dressed in suits or jeans with cowboy belts, on the phone, moving important papers around his desk. Best of all, it smelled like a mixture of coffee, files, and Dad.

"OK, Deena," Dad started. "Esther is off today. You sit at her desk. I have some filing you can do, mail you can open, and around lunch-time, we'll go out. I have work to do. I'll be in my office."

How can a chair with wheels be so much fun? How can an IBM Selectric typewriter be the best toy ever? And how can a room full of his client's samples that I don't need be fun to root through? But after only 20 minutes, the day seemed interminable. How can it only be 8:30 am? *Oh, my god*, I thought, *three hours till lunch? I'll never make it.* I opened and closed all the drawers, inspected pens, paper clips, and the staple remover. I made frequent visits to the coffee area where a bright yellow box of Domino sugar cubes sat open and was fair game for snacking. I happily consumed many! On to the Wheat Thins and still, it was only 9:00 am. *Oh, my god, this is the longest day ever. I'm so bored*, I thought.

I sauntered into my father's office. "Hi, Dad. So what time do you want to go to lunch?"

With his tortoiseshell readers at half-mast, he gave me an expression like I had just put a pile of aggravation on his desk. This was a facial expression our family and friends were all too familiar with. "Deena, don't you have something to do? We just got here! It's 9:00 am. I gave you filing and mail to open and you can answer the phone for me when it rings. I have work to do, honey," he explained.

I returned to my assigned station and filed a few things. I was not having fun.

9:10 am: "Dad, do you want me to refill your coffee?" Silence. I thought, *OK, I'm on my own here.* There was only one thing to do:

start typing. First I typed a fake library overdue notice addressed to my brother, Michael, indicating that he had checked out *Inherit the Wind* three years ago and never returned it, therefore at ten cents a day, he owed the library several hundred dollars. The second document I typed was from a fictitious executive named "Bob Sevvly" at the Playboy mansion, requesting my mother show up for a fake photo shoot. I had heard girls at school talking about the magazine and was curious about it. The letter included a request to bring a spatula and several other odd props from around the house. I had such a wry, offbeat sense of humor as a kid, nothing fazed me.

While most children my age were writing to Mary Poppins for autographs, I was typing letters from sleazy executives.

10:30 am: I plodded into my Dad's office and plopped in the chair. He leaned back with a half chuckle. "Deena, what are you doing?"

"Well, I was wondering when we were going to lunch?"

My father replied clearly amused but also frustrated, "How are you ever going to have a job someday if you can't stay busy?" I knew he had people to berate over the phone for unfulfilled invoices and other things to do, but I was running out of ideas and fake letters to write. (Ironically, when I started out in the work world, the first thing I did was open my desk drawer to mess around with paper clips and rearrange everything while checking the clock to see how soon I could go to lunch. I knew someday I'd have to work for myself. Being on someone else's clock clearly would not work for me!)

One more hour remaining until lunch: I decided to write a children's book and called it *The Mogglefroth Ignads,* about two different looking creatures, the Mogglefroth Ignads, and the Simbeckle Pigeon, learning to live in harmony. As I completed the final page, my father announced it was finally time to go. My father eventually read my outlandishly concocted letters and the children's book I created that day in his office. He laughed at the inventions of my wild mind and loved my book, which I eventually illustrated. He even championed my efforts writing and illustrating as I grew older.

At the restaurant, my father gently suggested that the next time I came for an office visit, I'd have to work. "I can't entertain you," he added. For years, he would tell the story of the day he took me to work and laugh. And for years, I would remember the excitement of being part of his world for an afternoon.

My father always loved going to his office, even after he retired. His office bustled with phone calls, mail arriving, and unpacking samples. He loved the "tumult" (as he called it) of conducting business.

When my husband, and I moved our fall prevention home safety company into a brand-new office space, my father was thrilled. At the age of 83, he began immediately fantasizing about how he could work for us. This was something that sounded fabulous in his mind, but in reality, it was a pain in the ass for him.

"Hey, if you guys need help up there, I can help," he said to me on a few different occasions. I was touched and honored that he was interested and willing.

"OK, if you want, you could answer the phone. We always need help with that," I offered.

"So, like, I'd have to talk to old people about falling?" he countered.

"Well, yeah, that's kind of what we do here, Dad," I said through my laughter. "OK, so no phones, but I do need assistance with inventory."

"So, like, you want me to count grab bars? How many bars do you have anyway?" he asked.

"Well, that's kind of it. We have a lot of clients who fall and need safety grab bars. What do you think? I'd love to have your help!"

"Well, Deena, I appreciate the offer. In all seriousness, how about I come up to the office, see everything, and then we can grab lunch?" he suggested.

"That sounds great. I'd love that. When would you like to come up? Let's make a date on the calendar."

"Well, I'm very busy. I'll need to check my calendar. I have to be out of town . . ." he trailed off. And just like that, in typical Dad fashion, as soon as you wanted or needed him, he would feign his lack of availability. This schtick began when I was a kid. If you had a special event or anything you wanted him to attend, his immediate response was always, "Well, I'll need to check my calendar. I think I'm out of town on that date." The family always knew he was kidding. I secretly think he just liked playing hard to get but loved being wanted.

When he finally committed to making a visit to our office, I decided to pick him up because he was no longer driving. Our date was set, and I felt a childlike exuberance. I knew one thing for certain: I wanted my dad to feel like he had a place at our office. He often mentioned popping in for a kibbitz. I wanted him to know, wherever I was, he always had a place to go (and he never needed a reason).

Drawing from my multiple visits to his office, I knew there were key components that needed to be part of his visit: coffee, donuts, and copies of the daily news—specifically, *The Wall Street Journal* and the *Arizona Republic*. I decided I would make my father an honorary member of our office by crafting him a personal coffee mug with his name on it.

As my car approached our office, he asked the name of the street we would turn on to get there. "Gelding, Dad. That's the street name," I told him.

"Oh, that's nice. Your office is on 'Horse without Balls' Street," he replied. "Make sure when you give your clients directions you tell them that!"

I escorted my father in, illuminating the space with a flick of a switch.

"Very nice, Deena. Can we go now?" he teased with a crooked smile.

"Oh my god, Dad!"

"What, Deena? We're here. I saw it. Is there anything else to see?" he asked, still goading me.

"Well, no, but I do have a couple of things I need to take care of." I am beyond gullible, and my father loved taking advantage of that fact.

"Just kidding, honey. Do what you need to do. I'm just happy to be with you. Your office is beautiful, and I'm really proud of you and Sandy and what you've built."

I presented him with his mug along with some donuts. "Dad, I got your favorite donuts. Would you like a cup of coffee to go with them?" I asked. He carefully opened the bag, looked in, and selected a cake donut. After taking a bite, he dropped it back in the bag. "Jesus, this is the worst donut I've ever had!"

"Sorry, Dad. How about some coffee? I have decaf," I offered.

"No, no coffee. I really don't drink coffee anymore," he announced.

Two strikes, and two newspapers to go.

The coffee and donuts were a bomb, and I could feel my excitement deflating. "OK, we can eat when we go to lunch. I got you newspapers you can read while I make a few calls," I said.

My father lifted the *Wall Street Journal* close to his eyes, grimaced, and put it back down.

"What's wrong?" I asked.

"Deena, this paper is from yesterday. I don't read yesterday's news," he declared.

"Well, what about the other paper?" I desperately implored.

"That's the *Arizona Republic*. I don't read that paper anymore!"

And just like that, everything I did to make my father feel at home failed to hit the mark (no pun intended!). For the next hour, my father became an observer of my work life. He would later share with me at lunch that he was impressed with how I handled the clients and colleagues and was sorry that I had not been older when he had his businesses, as he would have loved for us to work together. As things turned out, the thing that made my father feel most "at home" was being with me.

I never required my father's approval, but due to his nature, when he provided it, it was like being knighted.

Fleeting Thoughts
and Advice

"Hey Dad, I'm thinking of getting a new pair of cowboy boots; should I go up a size?" I asked my father one day. I was not always a person who sought advice from friends, siblings, or even my parents. However, throughout the years, I would seek input from my father regarding random situations or things I felt he had a level of expertise in. "Dad, I need to get a new car. What color do you think would be best?" "Dad, take a look my sales projections, what do you think?" My father for the most part always had answers and was happy to be a resource for his much-valued information. In fact, when I first moved to Chicago in my early 20s, he wrote me the following:

Dear Deena, you're off on a big adventure! I am confident that anything you decide to do will turn out well for you! Enjoy the experience and be careful. Anytime you feel like talking to a friend, call me! I Love You, Dad

Suffering from gastrointestinal issues (which I'm certain were born from living on my own in the city, where drunken hobos peed in ATM lobbies), I was told I needed a flex sigmoidoscope (basically, a garden hose disguised as a medical prop) procedure and was instructed to prep with a dosing of two Fleet enemas.

Since my father had had a lifetime of his own gastrointestinal issues, I could think of no other more perfect person to advise me on how to use a Fleet enema. Even though this was not your typical "dad" question, it didn't stop me from dialing his number.

"Hi, Dad. I'm calling because my doctor wants me to do a Fleet enema. (*With years of gastric issues formerly blamed on our Great Dane, I knew he was the guy to call*). Can you please tell me how to do this?"

"*Jesus, Deena!* Why the hell are you calling *me* for enema instructions?" he laughed.

"Well, Dad, I mean, you're kind of an expert with butt stuff."

"Deena, don't you have a friend you can call? What the hell am I supposed to do from here?"

"You're my dad! I need help!!!"

"Are you sure you can't get a hold of Mom? OK, OK, first read the directions, lay down on your bathroom floor, and don't leave until you finish going to the bathroom. Good luck, but don't let me know how it goes! Do me a favor, if you have a problem, call someone else. Good luck! Love you, bye!"

I knew he was the guy to call. His instructions paid off. No butts about it, I would never hear the end of it (*and I didn't!*)

Dating Interrogations and Unfiltered Declarations

"Anyone you date needs to meet me first. I need to make sure their intentions are good!" my father goaded me throughout my teenage years. He would alternate this by singing "Sweet Sixteen, teenage queen," which I hated.

Fathers are generally protective of their daughters when they enter the dating world. My father was no different. If Andrea or I were brave enough to share information about a boy we were interested in or possibly going out with, we would inadvertently expose ourselves to a forensic level of scrutiny.

In high school, I had a crush on a boy. He was literally my first date (if you don't count Elliott, my childhood sweetheart and best friend when I was six). While I was getting ready to be picked up for my first (and last) date with him, my father launched into his pre-date interrogation:

Dad: "What's your date's name? Well, we already know he's not Jewish. Where is he from?"

Me: "His name is Francisco. His family is Columbian. They have been living in the states for many years."

Dad: "What does his dad do? Does he work?" (What is it about fathers that they always want to know what other fathers do for a living?)

Me: "Daaaaaad! Oh my god, that's awful. They are such nice people. Why do you care what his father does? I'm not dating his dad!"

Dad: "Whatever, Deena. I don't care as long as you don't marry him or get pregnant."

Deena: "Oh my gooodddd! Dad!!!!"

And then there was my prom date. Knowing full well how worked up and nervous I was for my prom date (whose name I don't remember because the evening was *that* memorable) to pick me up, my father thought it would be amusing to remove his shoes and expose his hole-laden black knee socks. With his feet splayed on the coffee table, white undershirt, and beer in hand (he rarely drank or sported an undershirt), he looked like Archie Bunker. *My date is going to think I'm trailer trash!* I thought. *Bad time for stupid pranks, Dad!*

I have to admit that when my date picked me up, I was as taken aback and amused as my father was. My date showed up at the front door in chocolate brown tails and cowboy boots. I could hear my father laughing and thought I was going to spontaneously combust from the horror of it all. (It must also be noted I wore a very non-traditional prom dress—a Laura Ashley style, muslin tube top and matching lace skirt. I looked like an extra from *Little House on the Prairie!*)

Onlooking father, date with corsage in hand, Deena in a tube top—Houston, we have a problem. Thankfully my mother stepped in to the rescue. Starting the evening off with my date's hand inside my tube top in front of my father would have been a nightmare. My father said a few words to my date in between snorts of laughter. I couldn't get out of my house quickly enough.

Truth be known, I would have rather stayed home. It wasn't until years later that I was able to find the humor in both my father's antics and the prom date from hell. (Him: "I'd rather not spend money on valet parking, so let's just walk to the entrance of the dance." Me: "Oh, sure, no problem, I'd love my hair to look like it was blown around in a wind tunnel for our pictures.")

After seeing someone for a few months following college graduation, I thought I would bring him home to meet my parents. I wasn't super serious about my new boyfriend, but we were more than a fleeting story. I knew going in that this was going to be scary, especially given my father's loose cannon comments and unpredictable disposition.

My mom had indicated to keep it short as she had a headache. My father just wanted to watch TV. When my boyfriend arrived, we stood in the kitchen for a while, and everyone got briefly acquainted. My boyfriend was gregarious and insisted on continuing to share about himself with my parents.

The next day, I hesitantly asked my father what he thought.

"Jesus, that kid could talk the balls off a brass monkey. I thought he'd never leave!" was his reply.

Needless to say, that was the last time I ever brought him home.

The funny thing is, although my father's comments could be wry and crass, beneath them all, he knew what he was talking about. Initially critical, he saw things that took me longer to see. My incessant talker boyfriend was not the right fit for me. The prom date was from hell, and Francisco was a short-lived high school crush.

My father would say, "In all truth, if it's someone you love, all I care about is that they respect you, treat you well, and take care of you." His loving intentions always prevailed, even if he liked to make my dates feel uncomfortable for a good laugh. Actually, I believe I was the most uncomfortable. My dates never seemed to notice. They always thought he was hilarious.

My father was very kind to the boys I ended up dating for longer periods of time. If they were important to me, than they were important to him. Even so, those first introductions to my father were always interesting.

First, the introduction to my husband Sandy: I recall phoning home to share with my mother that I'd just had a blind date and was head-over-heels. Two weeks later, I phoned home again. My father answered, and I shouted into the phone, "I met this guy. We really hit it off, and *we're engaged!*" "Deena, I just talked to you, you didn't even know anyone!" he incredulously replied. Dad thought I was kidding him, but after much explanation of my whirlwind romance, his fears were semi-quenched and a visit was planned.

It's fairly nerve-wracking for a future son-in-law to meet his future father-in-law face-to-face. Still, my fiancé Sandy was very excited after what he'd heard about my parents. I had done everything but erect a highway billboard touting their praises!

My parents were still residing in Dayton, Ohio, and it was determined that an unassuming and low pressure mall outing with lunch would be an easy way to kick off our first meeting, even though my father detested the mall and thought only "the dregs of the earth" shopped there.

My parents took turns having one-on-one time with Sandy. First, my mom purchased for Sandy a bag of his favorite chocolate sweets, while Dad and I sat and awaited their return. "He seems very nice, Deena," Dad said, "but I'll check things out and let you know when we get back. He and I are going to have a talk."

God, if you can hear me, now is the time to listen. Please let it go well! I thought then, *Oh, shit, what's going to happen?* My father was probably just "ootzing" me, which was our watered-down Yiddish term for giving me a hard time.

Sandy and my father set off into the depths of the mall. Upon their return, there were smiles and laughter. Sandy recounted that in my father's attempt to "connect" he was bird-dogging with him. "Jesus, look at her, would ya?!" he'd say as women passed by. "Man-connecting" was not Sandy's style, thinking it both uncomfortable and hilarious. Sandy, not knowing whether to bond with my dad or be disloyal to me, rode the tide and laughed it off.

Later, Sandy asked my father privately for my hand in marriage. My father gave his blessing, feeling a real connection to Sandy. The deal was sealed with my father's final input: "Well, she's yours now, including all her credit card and dental bills!"

Second, the introduction to my daughter, Lindy. For my father and me, the second most important introduction to my father, was my daughter, Lindy. When I was several months pregnant, my parents drove to Cleveland, Ohio, where Sandy and I were living to take us shopping for some baby furniture.

My father, victim to a recent hair dye fiasco at the barber, was then sporting a disturbing and off-putting, reddish-brown hair color. His brother called him "Rusty." My father hated it. He was always a perfectionist about his appearance, but the baby store was no place for a ball cap or cowboy hat, so he combed his locks and off we went.

While we were shopping, a woman walked by my father, looked at him, and murmured quietly to her child, "Honey, stay with Mommy. Let's walk over here."

"Jesus, this fricking hair color!" Dad grumbled. "That lady thinks I'm a goddamn perv. I should have worn a hat!"

When Lindy was born, my mother was with me and Sandy in the birthing room. My in-laws and sister, Andrea, along with my father were on the other side of the door. My father had a cup to the door, "I can hear cries. The doctor said it's a girl!" He was beside himself with joy and came in to hold my new bundle of love. Dad and Lindy's bond was sealed on the spot.

A year later, my parents moved to Scottsdale, Arizona. Lindy and I would fly out to visit for ten days at a time. Dad taught Lindy the word "tuchus" (Yiddish for butt), and then he'd ask her, "Lindy, how long did it take you to fly to Arizona?"

She'd reply, "It *tuchus* a long time!" This became a running shtick with them for years to come.

Lindy and my father had the same connection as he and I did when I was little. Bright, playful, and loving, she engaged my father's inner kid. They played for hours. When we weren't visiting, he wrote her letters and phoned her. When Lindy was a toddler, we relocated to Scottsdale to be closer to Mom and Dad. Lindy and my father would go out for milkshakes. She would pop in for visits, and he attended her cello and singing recitals. "I could look at her for hours—the same way I love the mountains. I just can't get enough of her!" he'd always say.

Lindy loves to share the tale of the one day Grandpa picked her up from school. Earlier in the day, I had instructed him, "Here's what you do. The school has a loop around the parking lot. Pull through and stay in the line. It moves slowly as there are many children being picked up by their parents. Please be patient." Knowing I had to lecture him on patience concerned me. School pick up is the ultimate temper endurance test, one I wasn't sure he would pass!

Following my instructions, he threaded himself through the pick-up line and arrived at the front of Lindy's school, craning his neck in search of his pint-sized bounty. Lindy knew Grandpa was picking her up and smart as a whip always, she spotted his car and immediately hopped in.

"Hi Grandpa!" she bubbled.

"Hi Lindy!" Dad replied. "OK, honey, there's lots of traffic, buckle up and . . . Jesus, kid just walked in front of my freaking car!" he shouted.

"Graaaannndddpaaa!"

"Oh, sorry honey, this parking lot is crazy, I don't know how your mom or anyone else does it. The crossing guard isn't doing anything, people are walking everywhere, it's a freaking accident waiting to happen!" he barked.

"Grandpa, you just have to go slow and take your time. Mommy does it every day. It will be OK," Lindy advised, like a wise buddha. Slowly the lane opened up, and it was Dad's turn to get in. As he eased his car into the proper lane, he was cut off by a newbie, high school driver. "*Jerk-off, watch where you're going!*" he shouted angrily.

"*Graaaannndddpaaa*, that's not nice. I'm telling grandma!" Lindy feistily replied.

"Sweetie, I'm so sorry. Please forgive Grandpa, but this traffic is scary. I want to get you home safely like I promised. Will you accept my apologies? Can we keep this just between us?" he implored.

"It's okay, Grandpa. I won't tell," she gently said. "Grandpa?" she then asked.

"What, honey?" Grandpa replied.

"What's a jerk-off?" Lindy innocently inquired.

Dad began to laugh. "I'll tell you when you're older. It's not something you need to know or say. Just forget Grandpa said it, okay?"

"Okay, Grandpa."

Of course, Lindy immediately reported the "jerk-off" incident to me and any family member with ears. Everyone thought it was simultaneously hysterical and disturbing. "Dad, what were you think-ing? A jerk-off, really?" I asked aghast.

"God, Deena, I'm so embarrassed. It came flying out of my mouth and as soon as I said it, I regretted it. But the guy *was* a jerk-off. He cut me off and almost hit my goddamn car. That school parking lot is a death trap," he countered. Dad was being Dad.

My father never held back his comments from Lindy, nor did she with him. The two of them bantered with such joy and unconditional love. They got each other. He would make comments and ask about her dates, about school or other random topics. Lindy shot back, knowing how to stop him in his tracks (like mother like daughter!). Lindy kept video footage of all their goofing around, silly faces, and outings. This is a treasure trove of love she will always have.

My father's commentaries were not exclusive. He included every-one. Wherever and whenever. Whether it was my date, my sister's dates, or a bad dress that "looked like someone shot a couch," every-thing was fair game. In my early 50s, I would often meet my parents down at the mall and have a visit with them at their favorite coffee spot in front of Nordstrom's. If we weren't there, the grocery store, or In and Out for a burger and shake, my father and I could often be found at Costco. No matter where we went, my father's perpetual flying sparks of acerbic wit followed.

At some point during our frequent Costco excursions, he would undoubtedly launch into unsavory commentary about the people surrounding him. "Jesus, you think she could look in a mirror before she left the house?!" "Go ahead, eat another churro. Maybe it will go to your ass where the rest of them went!" My father, well-meaning in the quiet of his heart, was no match for the sound coming out of his mouth.

Although he softened a bit in his older age, when illness became part of his world, his anger and frustration permeated his filter.

I loved my father, but my skin would crawl when he blurted out his Don Rickle-esque barbs, which were audible to anyone within a thirty-foot radius. My father was not quiet when he had opinions to share. And boy did he love sharing them!

Following the barb-fest, we would perform our usual verbal dance, in which I'd implore him to see the error of his ways. The choreography to our dance included his jab, my dodge, and his last word, for example:

Dad: "Friggin' cashier. These kids don't know how to count change!"

Me: "Dad, he can hear you. He's just a kid!"

Dad: "I don't care how old he is, Deena. If he can't count change, for Christ's sake, then he shouldn't be a cashier!"

Me: "But Dad, he can hear you. It will make him feel bad. He's doing the best he can. Come on. Let's go."

Dad: "If he doesn't want to feel bad, then he shouldn't work with people."

In a nutshell, nothing the kid could do would save his soul in my father's eyes. First impressions were everything to my dad. If you screwed up, it was easy to fall quickly out of temporary favor. My father did not feel that his own children were "idiots" when they screwed up, but he had expectations of those in his orbit "getting it right." Deep down, my father never meant any malice, but clearly he was lacking some kind of tolerance, which made for a lot of interesting, uncomfortable, and hilarious moments. My mother became accustomed to letting all of this roll off her back.

I never got used to or accepted his strangely lovable impatience. Following each exchange, I would look at him with a penetrating gaze and say, "Daaaaaaaaad!"

"What, Deena?" he'd mutter through broken laughter.

"Dad, that's not nice. You should be more patient."

"I know, Deena. OK, OK." Then out came the last word: "These kids shouldn't be allowed to graduate school if they can't count money! When I was that kid's age, I worked in my father's tire store. He would have kicked my ass if I screwed anything up, let alone counting money! That's it, Deena. That's all I have to say about it." And just like that, the conversation was over.

Because I loved spending time with my father, we often went on outings. Of course, his insult jousting seemed to take place anywhere we went. Therefore, going to any public place with him was a fun and dangerous sport. Malls, restaurants, and large gatherings were all fodder for my father's acerbic wit.

Scene: *The mall where Dad sits awaiting my mother's return from her errands*

Me: "So, what's new, Dad?"

Dad: "Jesus, it looks like they let these people out of a circus. I've never seen so many fat people in one place in my life!"

Me: "Oh, my god, Dad, shhhhhhhh! It's the mall. People come from all over. If you look at me, you don't have to pay attention to other people, especially when they are aggravating you so much. Let's visit, I haven't seen you in a week."

Dad: "How could I not pay attention? OK, what's new? Nothing's new. This cookie from Nordstrom's bakery sucks. It's stale. I've got bad gas cramps and a brain freeze from this Frappacino, and I've been waiting for your mother for thirty minutes. You happy?"

Me: "It's not thaaaat bad, Dad." I say this with a crooked smile. "How bad is the cookie, really? If it was that bad, you wouldn't have eaten it. Are you still hungry?"

Dad: "Yea, a little bit. Why? You got something in your purse?"

Me: "I always have something in my purse!" I start unloading peanut butter crackers, chocolate, animal crackers. I'll be over the moon if I have something that will trip my dad's trigger.

Dad: "Jesus, Deena. How long has that stuff been in your purse? Those crackers look like I backed over them in the parking lot. No, thank you!"

Scene: at a restaurant, waiting to be seated

Dad: "Jesus, tell me they don't have a table. I'm looking at three empty tables now. That's bullshit!"

Me: "Dad, we just put our name in. The people waiting in line were all here before us. It won't be too long."

Dad (now seated): "Don't they wipe the menus? Christ, they're so sticky!" (says with pained face) *To waitress*: "What's your name? Debbie? Hi, Debbie. I'll have the hamburger, medium well, but don't overcook it so it tastes like rubber, French fries, and a Diet Coke. And I'm letting you know, if the chef screws up my hamburger, I'm sending it back, OK, Debbie?" *The food arrives*: "Debbie, you're very nice, but your chef sucks. This hamburger is too well-done. I can't eat this! You need to take this back."

Restaurants were historically a culinary pit of perpetual dissatisfaction for him. I wondered why he continued to go out with such frequency for breakfast, lunch, and dinners. My father's antics were a product of a painful childhood, a constant "do nothing right" hand slap from his father, and rigid family dynamics. In short, the world was "not getting it right."

I always managed to look past these behaviors because I innately understood my father and accepted whatever and however he was. I suppose there was part of me that almost worshipped my father. Michael and Andrea had visceral reactions equal to mine and also found humor at times; however, I believe I was willing to tolerate so much more from him and so many people in my life. This allowed me to enjoy him and all the parts of his personality. He was a person who just wanted to be loved, appreciated, listened to, and valued for his wisdom, guidance, and experience. I wonder if my father ever thought for a moment that his actions left as much of an impression on his children as his wisdom.

I believe that my lack of fear at his cardboard exterior allowed him to soften and for us to relate in ways that others couldn't. It was safe, it was OK, he was OK, and I loved him unconditionally as he did me. It was the mutual admiration society for certain. At heart, he was truly a kid and just wanted to have fun.

Here for the Calibration and Collaboration

Even before my father moved into the group home, his hearing was not his strong suit. Assisted with newly purchased Costco hearing aids, he heard fine for the most part. I would often take him to have them cleaned, repaired, or just for a good kibbitz at Costco's hearing aid counter, after which he always liked to cruise through the new releases in the book section.

Once in the group home, the hearings aids stopped working. This was an unexplained phenomenon we think was linked to Dad's not wanting to hear the caregivers so he could complain about them. I was willing to do literally anything my father asked if it would put a smile on his face. So began the hearing aid repair triathlon.

My instructions were detailed each time. God forbid I should screw anything up, so I listened to his instructions attentively. "Deena, something's wrong. The receiver is bent/ broken/needs batteries." "Deena, while you're there, tell them the other ear is not working." "Deena, I can't get them in my ears." "Deena, tell them they can replace them with a new set and see if they can do while you wait."

The probability of me remembering just two of these requests was highly doubtful.

Each time I returned, thankfully the hearing aids worked, and my father seemed pleased. And there came those familiar fireworks of joy, because for just a moment, he was healthy Dad, giving a directive, and getting what he needed. And me, getting it right and making him smile.

I had to take a moment, as I always do, to consider the humor and irony in everything. This was no different. "Deena, you're so shrill. Jesus, I can't turn these hearing aids down any lower!" my father would say during my visits. I was certain I still had PTSD from his father also saying it to me.

When my father passed away, my mother gave me my father's hearing aid set. Perhaps one day, I will trot off to Costco to have them cleaned and calibrated for myself. And, without a doubt, on my way out of Costco, I'll hear in my head, "Hey Dee, let's go look at the books."

Although there wasn't much levity to be found in my loud voice, in most situations, my father rarely lost grip of his wit and humor. Moments prior to his triple heart bypass surgery almost 20 years prior, I remember him providing multiple attending clinicians conflicting data regarding his height and weight. Confused and ultimately taking the mathematical average, they noted his stats.

My mother, sister, and I glanced at one another wondering what he was up to. We knew my father's motives were only to screw around with the heads of anyone who was willing to participate.

When he was taken to a hospital, his face devoid of color, he said to the triage nurse, "You think *I* look bad; you should see my brother." My mother awkwardly laughed at this wry comment regarding his long-deceased brother, Aaron.

Flirtations with nurses and jokes with physicians or anyone who would listen fueled Dad's energy to always be the source of delight and laughter in the room, when he wasn't making demands. And he never disappointed.

A few weeks into my dad's stay at his group home, he shared an idea that I purchase steno pads for us both to track funny experiences. (As with everything else, he was very specific that they were not to be spiral, composition, or legal pads; they *had* to be steno pads that opened from the top.) Each time we were together, we were to share what we had documented. I adored the idea because it meant that my father's wheels were still spinning, and he was having thoughts outside the periphery of his grim reality. My father, when well, was always crafting plans, ideas, and inventions. ("Deena, I had a great idea. You should invent a . . ." was a frequent phrase I heard.) I knew this one would easily come to fruition. His direction was explicit: we were to write our names on our respective pads and keep them close to the vest at all times.

Thrilled to do anything that brought a smile to his face, I purchased the supplies and reported back to him the following day, eager to embark on our secret comedy writing club! I anticipated how my father would turn lemons into a laughable tart beverage, as he documented his day-to-day trials and tribulations.

My father's first entry detailed the absurdity of a woman, older than himself, who had been sent in to bath him. "Jesus, she looked like she needs more help than me!" he wrote. Of course, he did not write about the fact that she dressed in fun, brightly colored accessories, had a spunky personality and calming disposition. He began to look forward to her visits. He prattled on about the ridiculousness of relying on caregivers to assist him in using the bathroom. "They don't know what the hell they were doing," he said. My father hated what was happening to him, and the humor he tried to extract from the situation deeply saddened me, but I never let on.

"OK, Deena, your turn. What do you have?"

What I had was an empty book. My humor was lost inside the heart of my father and nothing was funny to me. For the first time in my life, I felt devoid of humor. I explained it had been a busy work week, but I'd most surely have an entry by my next visit.

That was the first and last entry my father ever made in his book, as my father's condition worsened, his constitution weakened, and his motor skills waned.

My pad remains a blank reminder of moments unshared, stories untold and a very empty heart.

Evaporation of Struggling

During my father's first few weeks at the group home, he is feisty, vocal, and cognitively present. It seems that anger is his only vehicle to maintaining some kind of independence, and so he voices his concerns to anyone who will listen.

Despite the heartache I feel about his prolonged withering, I'm trying to bring lightness to our visits, anything that will allow him some moments of peace and joy. My father experiences severe chronic back pain by this time, and even small adjustments to his positioning in bed is untenable. His frustration, pain level, and weakness are zapping his desire for conversation, and so abbreviated dialogue between us is the norm.

I have always loved sitting as close as possible to my dad. Each visit, we hold hands and have snippets of conversation and occasionally tears of deep emotion.

After work one afternoon, I pay my daily visit, and without hesitation, sit on my father's bed next to him. Like being splashed with a bucket of ice water, I'm caught completely off guard when my father growls, "Deena, be careful. You're on my blankets. It's hurting me." I leap to my feet unsure of what feels more horrifying: that I have initiated his discomfort or that soft blankets are now a source of pain for my father.

I have come to understand that the more my father's body deteriorates, the more things cause him discomfort, even the slightest shift of clothing feels like razors to his skin and bones. Following this day, I never sit on his bed again.

My father's cantankerous complaints and feisty demeanor are signs that he is still in the fight. Sadly, I see a complete evaporation of struggling as he succumbs to the choices his body is now making on his behalf.

Along with his physical struggle, the family is witness to my father beginning his "checking out" process, which means disconnection and distance in normal communication whether on the phone or visiting in person. Prior to my father entering the group home, hospice would pay regular visits to my parents' house. My father's designated social worker provides my mother with a book, detailing the various phases my father will go through both physiologically and cognitively, so we will know what to expect. I remember having the privilege of speaking with my father's hospice social worker, whose spirit is a band-aid to my aching heart. My father is seated on his corner of the couch, my mother on the opposite side, and the social worker in the middle. I sit across from my father in his parked transport chair, vowing to keep silent so that my father feels no intrusion into this deeply personal space we now all fill.

"Marc, how are you doing? How do you feel?" his social worker asks.

"Fine, I'm fine. How do I feel? How do you think I feel? I don't want to answer these questions. I'm not doing this," he responds with an angry face.

"Marc, I know you are frustrated, but it's important you talk about your feelings. It's important for you, Joan, and your family. You are dying, and you are going to have feelings about that," she gently encourages.

A cold river of fear, imminent loss, and horror seared my veins and rendered me breathless, a state I'd come to be in often throughout his illness. This is the first time anyone tells my father, to his face, in my presence, that he is dying. Everyone one knows it, including him, but nary a word is spoken in his presence. A deafening, heavy silence fills the room. My mother sits quietly, waiting to see if my father will respond. No response comes. With that, the social worker understands my father's silence speaks volumes, so she stands, makes her information available to my mother and myself and leaves.

These kinds of flashbacks catapult me far away while I sit with him in his room in the group home. As I look at my father in his bed, he too is also far away, his disconnection is his process, his trek toward leaving. I know it is too painful for him to stay connected. It makes it harder for him to leave, yet I long for contact with him—a touch of the cheek, anything.

I opt to try my luck at the end of one of our visits by asking if I can give him a kiss. I miss his stubbly face against mine. I am elated when he nods yes, with just a hint of a sweet grin. I plant my love on his cheek and say, "I'm always so excited to see you. I love spending time with you."

"I just love being around your karma," he replies. This is an interesting choice of words coming from my conservative father. On a good day, in good health, my father's private nature made him a man of few words, so any words escaping now are pure gems to me.

With that, I leave, my chest tight with love and sadness like a tangled ball of yarn, as I desperately try to breathe while walking to my car. Catching my breath becomes the new normal for me.

I Hope You Don't Mind

A month has passed since my father moved into his group home, and as I have for many days, I'm stopping by to visit him. News is breaking of a worsening pandemic in the country, which will eventually affect our family's ability to visit him.

"Hi Dee," my father whispers as I entered his room.

"Hi, Dad, how are you doing today?"

Observing my father, I notice he is weak and undernourished due to his illness and cloudy from medication. He already looks depleted from our brief exchange. Our "new routine" was just being together, without conversation or keeping it minimal at best.

An avid news watcher, my father knows of the pandemic and is now leery of touching or even a kiss on the cheek. Our visits are sterile, with me taking a seat on the couch adjacent to his bed. It's incredible how time can simultaneously seem slow and fast. At first, the starkness of his new home was harsh. Days pass. New home becomes normal. Worsening condition becomes new. Month passes. Sitting what seems miles away from my father becomes normal. More time will pass, and his passing will be anything but normal or OK.

"I hope you don't mind," he whispers, "but I really don't feel like talking, OK, honey?"

"Of course, Dad, it's OK. I just came to be with you. How about I stay for just a few minutes?"

He nods.

As we sit in silence, my father gazes at the television while I drink him in, worried to lose a split second of having him in my life. His now hollowed cheeks, hoarse voice, and slight frame are still a force in the room. I can feel his fight to stay alive. His umbilical cord of lifeblood remains attached to Mom, Michael, Andrea, myself, and his grandkids. In essence, family is a tremendous source of joy and drive in my father's life. He fights daily to not say goodbye and leave us.

I will continue to visit daily until we are no longer permitted in-person visits. I feel like my father is being taken from me prematurely because of the restrictions the pandemic has caused. Even worse and most importantly, I don't want him to feel alone or scared in his waning days. It's a nightmare that we have no choice but to navigate, like so many other families dealing with the same painful predicament. Because my mother is immunocompromised from nonaggressive lung cancer, she and Dad are forced to remain in their respective safe havens for the best interest of each other's well-being. As fate will have it, my father until the very end of his days is able to see no one in person.

But before this happened, we are able to FaceTime with him— thank God! Of course there are many hang up calls, hip dials, and confusing moments, but our family will gladly take whatever connections we can muster.

After many weeks, my father senses his cognitive abilities are dramatically shifting and is requesting that my mother arrange a family Zoom meeting, grandkids and all. Andrea is permitted with mask, gloves, and a laptop into my father's room to facilitate this.

We quietly awaited the "ding" that heralds my father joining the meeting. There in a one-inch frame is the face of the man we all adore. If you knew our family, you would not anticipate that we could be quiet when gathered together. We are a noisy, interrupting gaggle, always excited to connect with one another. But this moment, you can hear a pin drop. We wait silently and deferentially for the patriarch to speak.

In classic Dad style, he utters, "Why is everyone so quiet? Why is no one talking?" Although mildly amusing, it is piercingly sad that he doesn't seem to understand the gravity of what we were all experiencing. He checks his memory and performs a spontaneous roll call, to which everyone softly replies, "Hi, Grandpa" or "Hi, Dad."

My father then states, "Well, we all know what's going on here. I've said goodbye a hundred times, and I don't want to do it again. I just wanted to say hi to everybody." And just like that, my father ends his portion of the call. Our family is at an unprecedented loss for words.

We understood that a large lump of emotion has choked my father's ability to communicate any further. Nothing and everything has been said in those brief moments. It would be the last time the family collectively sees him.

Whether visiting or FaceTiming, or connecting in any other way, toward the end of my father's life, "I hope you don't mind" becomes a metaphor for him checking out. The more he is able to disconnect from the loves of his life, the easier it is for him to take leave of the earth. And so, our need to connect is bittersweet, as he still longs for it, but it causes him great anguish and difficulty. Ultimately, we are respectful of his need to begin his journey, while silently knowing we are embarking on ours, minus this incredible soul who has impacted each of our lives.

"OK, Little Bird"

Three months following Dad's move into the group home, the COVID-19 pandemic rages on, and a nationwide quarantine is mandated, residentially and commercially. My world as I know it is flipped on its end, as is everyone else's. Our family is one of hundreds experiencing the same set of unimaginable circumstances. The Centers for Disease Control mandate no visitation policies in nursing home facilities. Simply stated, everyone is forced to stay in their homes. Cold runs through me as I realize I have no way to get to my father, and given his poor health, I'm terrified that time and absence will take him away before I have the chance to see him once again. I'm hell bent on finding a safe loophole.

Technology is the salt to my corn, and my family is able to start FaceTiming with Dad intermittently during his isolation in the group home, due to the pandemic. Historically, anything having to do with technology was not his favorite. My father was not alone; so many elderly struggle with the unending advancements in technology—texting, FaceTiming, and every changing phone functionality. There are the accidental midnight calls, when he frantically tries to reach family members when he wakes up scared and alone in his room. Gabriel tells my mother about my father's hallucination-filled evenings caused from the morphine he's on. At one point, my father insists he's late for a meeting. Compassionately, Gabriel wheels him into the main lobby and says, "Here, Marc, here you go." After a few moments, he's calmed from his nocturnal frenzy and quietly taken back to bed.

My father knows he's dying, and at one point, my brother Michael asks him, "Are you afraid?"

My father replies, "No, I'm not afraid. I just don't know how to die. I'm just waiting for it to happen."

My father communicates to me in those waning days that the only thing that keeps him fighting is the family. This is a testament to his love and devotion.

After two months of observing the non-visitation restrictions, I learn I'm able to visit my father through the screen of his private patio. I think my heart will burst from utter joy that I'm finally allowed to see him.

Knowing he craves a taste of home, I go to task crafting a peanut butter and jelly sandwich on white bread (his favorite) portioned into four squares. I add applesauce and Lay's potato chips (his other favorite), fantasizing that my paper plate feast will be a home run. Along the way, I stop to pick up his favorite McDonald's vanilla milkshake to accompany his lunch. I'm instructed upon arrival to drop off the food at the front desk, so Lisa, the nurse, can take the food to his room, as visitation is still prohibited inside.

Hi Dad,

Here is a homemade, peanut butter and jelly sandwich – no crust, on white bread I made for you! And, 4 Oreo thins, a little bag of Doritos and a Cinnamon applesauce for a snack later if you like.

I miss you so much and think about you ALL the time. I'm beyond excited that I get to see you today. I know it's just from the door, but thrilled we can lay eyes on each other and have a quick visit. I'm filling this note with tons of love from me to you!!!!!!!

I love you!!!!!!!
Deena

I round the corner to my father's private patio, my heart pounding so hard in my chest, I think it will knock me over. As instructed, I call Lisa to signal my arrival. She's in my father's room while I stand on the other side of the screened door. I hear her say, "Marc, your daughter is here. Do you want to sit up?" There is a moment of silence and then a rustling noise. "Deena," she says, "he wants to come to the door." As if I'm not already breathless with excitement, I feel awestruck that he's choosing to exert whatever energy he has to get out of bed and see me. He hasn't had the ability to adjust his positioning or even left his bed in weeks for anything other than assisted trips to the bathroom.

Exhausted and drained of color from his transfer from bed, my father sits hunched in his chair, his arm dangling lifelessly from the plastic armrest. Suddenly, I begin to see him slump. His blood pressure plummets. I watch him begin to pass out. Lisa rouses him and gets him to drink his milkshake as he rights himself in his chair.

The pain of seeing my father in such a state goes beyond anything I've ever known. The fact that he's willing to endure so much is simultaneously incredible and gut-wrenching. This is the only way he can show his love for me, as his strength to form words is almost nil.

Here we are, finally. Time is of the essence as I can see he is completely wiped out already. I say to him, "Hi Dad, thank you for getting out of bed for me. I know it hurts to move. Oh my god, it's *so* good to see you. I miss you *so* much." I know better than to ask him how he's doing, as it's obvious.

He nods, still panting from the exertion. His spindly elbows rest on the handles of his transport chair as he hangs his head and stares at the ground. Then he asks in a raspy, breathless voice, "How is everybody? How's Lindy?" I catch him up as quickly as possible, sensing the limit to his concentration and ability to hold himself up.

During our brief visit, he intermittently sips on his cold milkshake. He'll never be able to eat the peanut butter and jelly sandwich, which I understand. I don't care; I'm just over the moon to see him in person.

"Deena, see the frog?" With the slightest movement of his finger, he directs my gaze to the ground next to my chair where a large cement frog sits. Despite all his pain and suffering, he's playing with me.

After a long gap of silence, he says, "OK, little bird." I know this heralds the end of our brief meeting and his need to get back in bed. This is a phrase he's never uttered in his life to me before, but one that has more impact than any I've known. I'm no longer the little monkey with moppy hair dangling in her eyes. I'm not a toddler-sized "peanut," or even "baby girl," which seems ill-fitted to this moment. Once "little bird" escapes my father's lips, I know in the deepest sadness of my soul he's letting go. Letting himself go. Letting me go. Telling me it's time to fly. My father's faint and feathery words set in motion the surreal undoing of my world as I know it. In time, they will become the very underpinnings of my strength. In all the loved-filled exchanges between us, never has he uttered such a meaningful and transformative phrase.

And with that, we exchange I love yous, and Lisa wheels him back to bed. I feel like I can't breathe yet again. I'm breathless with love, breathless with heartache, and breathless at the pain he's willing to endure for me, for himself, just to stay on "this side of the grass," as he always puts it. I'm witnessing in real time the existential loss of my father, the most devastating loss of my life. "Little bird, little bird, little bird" is what I will hear in my head all the way home and for the rest of forever.

Later that day, I receive the following voicemail from my father: *"Hi Deena. It's Dad. I'm on my way to go night-night. I felt bad because I thought I hurt your feelings today. I'm so very, very sorry. I love you so, so much, and I enjoyed seeing you and I always will. OK, so you understand the food thing, and I want you to know it had nothing to do with loving you. OK, so I'm going night-night now, and I'll talk to you tomorrow. Love you. Bye."*

Gravelly Love at the End of the Road

Throughout years of family dinners and gatherings, my father would share his stories. Sometimes through laughter so intense, he'd tell snippets through squinted eyes filled with tears. The family was always in awe at how much joy he got when sharing stories about his brother, or about being a Navy Medic, or funny stories about his father. Dad use to giggle telling Mom, Michael, Andrea, and I how he would rearrange office supplies and knickknacks on his brother's desk when they were in business years ago. Particular about having an uber-organized desktop, my father's brother, Aaron, would feverishly work to return all pieces and parts to their original location, while he and my father laughed through it all.

It wasn't until later in life that my father began sharing personal stories, and Sunday family dinners became a regular event. We rotated houses and menus for these once-in-a-lifetime moments during which priceless memories were created. Family dinner nights began before my father became ill, but became regular and much anticipated during his decline.

For an hour, there were no thoughts of terminal health problems, no pain, or fears of my father's impending absence. News of the day, politics, children, grandchildren, and just happenstance dialogue carried the meal from one week to the next.

It was hard to believe that soon his designated chair at the dinner table would be hollowed of his presence. With that thought came a stream of places where the weight of his existence played out: the corner of the couch, the gray den recliner, his office chair, and the recliner in my family room. As if set in cement, these were my father's outposts. When I thought of their impending vacancies, I felt as if a zephyr of life was being knocked out of me.

The family learned more about my father in his final months than we had all the years prior. He opened up, was candid, emotional and, as always, he kidded. But the interchanges became fewer, as his ability to be present lessened.

I would continue to do what I had always done, just be there. It was so difficult for me to see how physically changed my father had become. I reflected on all the severe, near-death health issues he had overcome.

Several years prior to his passing, he was diagnosed with a rare form of cancer called Burkett's Lymphoma. His physician implored my mother to get her "affairs in order." Shell shocked and caught completely unprepared, I was at a loss for words around my dad. I was told he would die and didn't know what to say or do. All I could muster was, "Everything will be OK, Dad."

He turned to me and replied, "No Deena, everything is not going to be OK. You can't say that to people because sometimes things are not OK, and it doesn't make them feel better. I know what's happening to me. That's the reality. It is what it is. So, if you want to say something, you can just say, 'I'm here for you, or if you need anything.' I know you're just trying to be supportive, but it's important for you to know if you are going to try to understand where I'm at."

Given his prognosis, he also felt he needed closure and although uncomfortable, began sharing his "closing remarks" with me, which were overwhelming and hard to hear but so touching and comforting; I'm glad he shared them with me. "Deena, I want you to know, that if my world stopped tomorrow, I'm grateful for your mom, our family, and the life I've had. I couldn't ask for anything more. I want you to know I'm so proud of you and everything you have done and the young woman you've become. You have a beautiful life, and it makes me feel good to know that you're taken care of. Sandy makes a wonderful life for you, and I'm so proud of him too and the life you've built together. You've raised a wonderful child. Lindy is the best. I love her so much!"

I never forgot his lesson. I understood it, internalized it, and continued to be there for him. Ironically, he ended up being "OK," as he beat the odds of that particular terminal diagnosis, along with several others that would come to pass over the next few years. I remember always thinking I should get him a cape because he truly was a superhero to me. He fought through open heart surgery, two bouts of lung cancer, prostate cancer, stenosis in his back, and cachexia, which he ultimately succumbed to.

My father's impact on me that afternoon has helped me cope with his eventual loss. He showed me how to move through cold reality because sometimes you don't have choices. And he showed me appreciation, gratitude, and resolve. I'd like to think wherever he is now, he's wearing a red-lined cape that's fluttering in the wind. He will always be my superhero.

Bad Gifts and Random Laughs

Throughout my childhood and adulthood, it has not been unusual for me to have spacey, airhead moments. Even when I was younger, I was fearless and did things that would make my family's jaw drop. Never harmful, never mean spirited, just off the rails kind of stuff.

When I was eight years old, I recall being dropped at the mall with my sister and brother. Together we would shop with money we barely had. On this particular occasion, I had a mission: I needed a birthday gift for my father, and no mundane gift would suffice.

I went to task dragging my siblings in and out of stores, pit-stopping at Hot Sam soft pretzels in between to fuel my search. As I often did, I landed in Spencer's, an off-beat, often inappropriate gift store. After much searching through the aisles, I landed on the perfect gift. My father was a smoker for years, so I was trying to figure out smoking-related gifts for him. A twisted and disturbing reality at that time. Michael, Andrea, and I hated cigarettes and cigarette smoke, particularly in the car. On what planet is it OK to treat your moving vehicle like a brisket smoker with your kids in the back?! It was a time in our country when smoking was en vogue. This occasion would be no different. I purchased an accompanying card and anxiously awaited my father's big day.

My mom, brother, sister, and I gathered in the family room, and I sat at my father's feet, as always, brimming with excitement as he opened his birthday card from me, which said:

Card Front: *If you borrow from Peter to pay back Paul, Peter won't be very happy.*

Card Inside: *Now I ask you, who can have a happy birthday with a sore Peter?*

My father closed the card and burst out laughing. "Jesus, Deena! Where did you get this? This is the kind of card you give your father?" He was appalled and delighted in the same moment.

My brother grumbled, "If I gave that card to Dad, I'd be grounded for the rest of my childhood!"

Next was the gift! My father carefully unwrapped the little box. At this point, I could see he was a little hesitant, based on the card I had just given him. Out he pulled a pink, ceramic sculpture of a toilet with the lid up, inscribed "Stick Your Ash Here." He could barely speak he was laughing so hard. He turned it around to show the rest of the family. "Deena, what is it?" they all asked.

"It's an ashtray for Dad!" I replied jubilantly.

The following year, I returned to Spencer's Gifts and purchased a pair of tan underwear briefs for my father, which featured naked cartoon caveman running around the perimeter of the underwear. Years later, I would ask him why they were still in his drawer if he had never worn them. He simply laughed and said, "I'm not wearing those, but it was a gift from you, and I felt bad, so I didn't want to get rid of them." My dad didn't care about the gift, but he did about the gesture.

In my early 20s, I was making a modest living as a secretary. I happened upon a garden center from which I purchased a beautiful oversized "fork and spoon" set for my parents' anniversary. As usual, I was beyond thrilled at the cleverness and tasteful nature of my gift.

My mom would often let my father open the packages first. As my father lifted the lid on the box and pulled out the oversized "utensils," he began to laugh. "Deena, Jesus! How big do you think my mouth is?" he said.

"What do you mean?" I replied genuinely concerned.

"What are these? Where did you get them?" he asked.

"I got them at a garden gift store. They are salad servers."

"Deena, these are not salad servers. They are gardening tools. Why would a garden center sell salad servers? Jesus! Nice, Mom and I will serve salad with the garden tools. Thank you, that was very thoughtful!"

My gift faux pas comedy tour continued late into my 20s, when I was living in Chicago. I spent a lot time in the men's section of the local department store looking for a birthday gift for my father, when I happened upon a handsome pair of men's shorts. A week later, my phone rang.

Dad: "Hi, Deena."

Me: "Hi, Dad!"

Dad: "Deena, in your life, have you ever seen me wear anything with an elastic waistband?"

Me: "Huh?"

Dad: "Deena, first, I appreciate the thought. You shouldn't be spending your money on me, but honey, you sent me *shorts*. I can't wear these. They have an elastic waistband. I *don't* wear elastic. I've *never* worn elastic. Where did you get these, and can you return them?"

Me: "Oh, yeah, I can return them. I didn't know that."

Dad: "By the way, please don't buy me shorts. I don't wear those either."

When I wasn't intentionally buying ridiculous gifts, my blunders would extend into cooking when Dad came to our house to eat.

Understanding my father needed to be mindful of his sugar intake, I made baked apples for dessert. Like a proud peacock, I deposited my father's Apple Brown Betty in front of him and took my seat.

Making a face, he asked, "Deena, what is this?"

"Oh, it's Apple Brown Betty. You mentioned the only thing you could eat was Apple Brown Betty, so I made it for you!"

"Deena, I never in my life told you that. I've never even heard of Apple Brown Betty. What's in this?"

"I peeled apples and put cinnamon on them and baked it. Is it good?"

"Deena, I love you and appreciate the thought and the effort, but I can't eat this. It tastes terrible, and for the record, I've never heard of Apple Brown Betty. You made that up!"

Well, for the record, I'm uncertain as to where that name came from, but I'm pretty sure it was from my dad, despite his protestations.

Father's Day

It's Father's Day and like every other day this week, hospice is paying a visit to my father at his group home to check his vitals and life status. Earlier in the week, with mild uncertainty, the hospice representative indicated that clearly my father's death was imminent, but that he still seemed to be "holding on." Yet, all signs point to definite changes in his respiration, as well as his food and liquid intake and responsiveness.

We know the clock is ticking but don't know when the hands will stop for my father. In typical Dad fashion, there's no way he's going to screw up a perfectly good holiday for his family. (I feel the need to mention here that on several previous Father's Days, he received unwanted Henley shirts. I think he's holding out one more day to see if he gets another one, so he can taunt us about his ever growing Henley collection.)

After a long day, Mom eventually goes home for much-needed rest. Andrea has also been at my father's side since the early hours of the morning, and she, too, dearly needs sleep, so she goes home as well. I opt to stay because I'm concerned that my father might leave us while he's unattended.

As the sun sets and darkness begins filling in the corners of the sky, a chill takes over my father's room. Perhaps this is the chill of my father's mortality overtaking me. I slip into my father's closet and select a beautiful, soft, corduroy shirt (it's one I purchased for him a few years prior). It smells of his sweetness. I wrap the oversized shirt around me and sit on the couch.

There's no question that during the course of the day, my father's facial features have become more waxen and taut. His fixed upward gaze seems somehow even more distant and haunting to me.

It's clear to me that my father's body is tired of fighting. Fighting to breathe. Fighting to hear. Fighting the pain in his bones.

I step once again into my father's closet so as not to disturb his peace, and FaceTime my brother. As always, I provide updates and pertinent information on his status. Michael, his wife and I chat briefly, and then Michael says, "Hey, Deena, put the phone up and flip the camera. I want to say happy Father's Day to Dad."

"Uh, Michael, I don't think that's a good idea. You haven't really seen him. He doesn't look good."

"Yeah, Deena, I know, because he's dying," Michael says irreverently.

"No, seriously Michael, I'm concerned. I really don't think this is a good idea. I'm worried it's going to be upsetting."

"Deena, come on, OK? I just want to say happy Father's Day to Dad. I want him to hear my voice. It's fine."

I quietly pad over to the foot of my father's bed and flip the camera. As Michael begins to say, "Happy Father's Day, Dad," his voice cracks, and I immediately turn the phone around. In choked sputters, Michael says, "I gotta go. I can't talk."

I know Michael saw a horror he does not wish to have emblazoned on his mind: his father in the cloak of death. Yet I know in Michael's heart, he knows that Dad heard his Father's Day wishes one last time, which is what he wanted.

Following the call, I return to the couch. The only light in the room comes from a small, side lamp. Darkness deepens, shadows sharpen, and I feel incredibly frightened. I wanted to look at my father, but his face scares me. His once full cheeks are now hollowed and slack. I curl up into a fetal position, bound tightly in his shirt, and stare at the foot of his bed. I text Michael, "Michael, I'm so frightened. I don't want to leave Dad. What if I'm the last family member, I leave, and he dies alone?"

"It's OK, you don't have to stay there. Can you get someone to pick you up?" Michael asks.

"I'm so scared. I don't know what to do."

"Deena, he's knows you've been there. You are not responsible . . . I couldn't sit there. I would be scared, too. Go home and get some rest. It's OK."

No sooner do I finish texting Michael than Gabriel thankfully shows up. He also tells me to go home, and that he'll call if anything happens.

At 9:45 pm, I stride to my car, wearing my father's shirt. Terror, pain, and penetrating sadness envelop and overwhelm me. An uncontrollable cry escapes from my throat. The icy tentacles of reality grip me that my father is about to die. How am I going to get home let alone get through the next day?

June 22, 2021

Late morning, I write, "Dear Rabbi, I'm texting you to make you aware that hospice expects my father to pass today. As promised, I will be in touch with final details." Mom, Andrea, and I take turns holding vigil over Dad. We spend hours and hours sitting, watching, and waiting. We note signs such as mottling of his skin, his slower respiration rate, and his rumbling, panting breaths. Hospice has schooled the family on these signs that indicate his imminent death.

Having stayed late into the early evening on Father's Day, I'm emotionally and physically drained, so knowing my mom and Andrea are at my dad's side beginning early the next morning, I sleep in and regroup at home. Midday I return to my father, while Mom and Andrea are still there. Andrea and I step out of the room momentarily to give my mom the chance to say a private goodbye to my father, so she can go home and get some rest.

Now carrying the torch for the remainder of the day, Andrea and I take our places on the "shitty" couch that has been our daily perch for what seems an ephemeral eternity. We watch. We wait. We exchange purse snacks and intermittent conversation, but it's scrambled dialogue that can only take place in the surreal environs of a dying parent. Like kindred spirits, she and I squirrel away to the closet where, in order to snack, we have to rustle bags and loudly crunch. If he could talk now, he mostly surely would bark, "*What the hell is so loud? What are you eating? It sounds like a pack of goddamn monkeys in there! Jesus, I'm trying to die. Can you give me a freakin' break?!*" The snacks provide us with a brief respite from the pangs of sadness and a much needed fleeting relief from the unbearable darkness in our hearts. It's something only Andrea and I understand.

Gabriel stops in to check on my father. He gently touches his hand, examines his skin, and lastly checks the reading on the pulse oximeter. He repeats this twice as he's unable to get a reading. Finally, on the third attempt, he notes respiration in the 70s and looks at us gently but directly. "Of course, your dad is a fighter," he says, "so knowing him, it is possible this could go on for another day or so. There's no way to know. When the respiration is this low, it usually means they're close."

Andrea and I have already been at our father's side for several hours. With day turning to evening, we begin discussing our plans for the next day. As I sit facing Andrea, I'm overtaken by an uncontrollable shaking. My entire body starts trembling. "Andrea, something's happening! It's happening," I blurt out as I grab her by the arms. "It's happening! I can feel it! I can't stop shaking!" Andrea grabs ahold of me for what seems like an eternity but is only a few moments.

"It's OK. Nothing's happening," she says.

We turn to look at my father, and a different kind of stillness has overtaken him. "Oh, my god, Andrea. Oh, my god, I think he's gone!" Knowing that with his slowed respiration, Dad can go longer between breaths, we watch his chest, waiting for the familiar panting we had become accustomed to over the past few days. Nothing comes. Ever. Not one additional breath. Our father has died. Simultaneously, my involuntary convulsive shuddering stops. My head feels like it's going to explode. Oh, my god, my father died. Oh my god, *my father died*! Oh, my god, I feel like I just lost my soul. My insides feel barren and black. I will forever feel that in the very moments of his passing, he passed through me as our ultimate act together, he's letting me be a part of his final departure.

And just like that, my dad is gone. My best friend. The guy who was the constant source of illuminating energy. I feel hollowed, empty, and bereft with the deepest pain I've ever known. We all expected this, but preparing for how you feel when it happens is another story.

Back to reality, Andrea and I have to kick into gear. At 7:01 pm, my father passed away. At 7:02 pm, Andrea calls our mother to share the news. In that same moment, my husband Sandy and Andrea's husband Lee show up. Shell shocked, we go into action, as Mom needs us, and there is much to be done. Sandy and I go to Mom's, and Andrea and Lee stay behind to orchestrate the final transport of my father and the official call of the time of death.

Prior to leaving my father's room, I turn to glance at him one last time. For the first time in days, his pupils begin to rapidly reduce in size, his eyelids slowly closing in his last act of life. I cannot kiss him goodbye for fear that I'll never let him go. So, I leave because it's the only way I know how to separate from someone who is such a part of me that I now feel torn and shattered inside.

The ride to my mother's house is silent. Everything seems so stony and cold. The cactus and houses I've driven past a hundred times all look and seem as if the color has been drained out. This is because life is now different. It's weird to think that hours earlier when I saw those things, I had a father. Now, same things, no father. Every day from now on will be a repeat of the same. I'll collapse later (or maybe I won't).

I believe two things: My father did not want his daughters to bear witness to his final departure. He was always private and forever "out of towning." Secondly, there is no question in my mind that my father's energy passed through me. I've never before or since experienced a trembling the likes of what I went through the very moment my father left us. It came on strong and stopped on a dime. I know in my heart and have always felt it since the moment the shaking ceased that some of his energy stayed within me. I feel his presence daily.

To be with a loved one as they pass from this life is a great honor. Hospice will tell you that the last of the senses to depart is hearing, so we know that Dad could hear me and my sister in his room, so he knew he was not alone. I believe with all my heart that when my mom said goodbye to him that very afternoon, gently touching his face the way he loved, it was the permission and closure he needed to finish his work on this earth. I believe he didn't want her present when he left, his last act of taking care of her.

I can never erase the sights, sounds, and overwhelming moments that transpired that afternoon. If you had asked me a few years prior about being with my father when he was dying, I would have thought it an impossibility. That I was too weak or fragile to handle it. I believe my family often wondered if I would morph into a pile of salt when this moment came to pass. I often wondered the same.

I know this to be a great untruth, as I was raised strong and capable of weathering any storm. Dad said it was part of life, so I had to be part of his death. It was OK, it was necessary, and it was a gift. He was freed from the shackles of pain and suffering. And although I lost the greatest treasure in my life, he walks with me, lives inside of me, my daughter, and in every member of our family. His presence is very much with us all.

The Necessary
Finality of It All

My father passed away on June 22, 2021. The funeral
was planned for two days later, on June 24th. As my parents had connections to the temple that Sandy, Lindy, and I had been closely affil-
iated with for years, our rabbi was honored to officiate my father's
funeral proceedings.

Given the pandemic, surreal protocols were put in place. With
a handful of family present but six feet apart and masked, connected
by navy blue satin strands of ribbon, we sat and watched as my father
received his long-coveted military tribute (something he would have
been thrilled to know he received, as he always would comment on
ones he had attended for friends) and a traditional reform Jewish
service. I remember staring deeply into my rabbi's eyes, imploring the
divinity out of him to release me from the unbearable pain I was experiencing. No matter how hard I stared, the impossible did not happen.
I could not be shaken from the vision of a flag-draped coffin which
had held my father's body. Later I learned from my sister and mother
that we all had felt my father's essence was very much departed from
that scene (classic Dad, he probably needed to be "out of town"). The

service was beautiful, simple, and abbreviated as my father would have liked. The rabbi had deftly captured his essence, impact, and legacy. My brother, due to the risk pandemic travel could potentially cause or his prior health issues, was unable to attend, and so with the saving grace of technology, he and his family did so via FaceTime. It mattered not whether we were there in person or pixels; my father had received the final respects and love he deserved. Following the funeral, I reached out to the rabbi via email:

"Dear Rabbi, how do you thank someone for finding a way to take you through the most painful pain and loss and find light in its path? That's what you did for our family. For those family absent and far, you brought them into the fold, including and making them feel equally surrounded by love. Every person in my family adores you. Your spirit, your incredible compassion, and how you beautifully synthesized and gathered from each of us pieces of my father, sharing a bouquet of memories and essence of his spirit and impact. My mother felt comfort in your presence, words, and officiating. She loved the service and felt it captured him and the lightness of him as well.

I have to say, as a branch of god's tree, during the funeral I kept looking at you with piercing pain and loss, hoping something from your connection to the divine would help me. In doing so, I realized you were *that* very connection that helped me. And so how do I thank you for that? I may reach out soon for council as I navigate the deep waters of my grief.

Quieted and forever grateful. Thank you, thank you, thank you. Deena"

The evening of my father's passing, a Zoom memorial was held. On our respective computer screens, family and friends gathered from near and far. Zoom memorials were becoming the norm during the pandemic as a means for so many families to honor their loved ones.

Memories and stories filled with love and laughter poured from more than thirty of his grandchildren, children, and friends. It was clear my father had unequivocally impacted so many lives. Drained of life and what little emotion I had left, I formally honored my father one last time:

". . . In the recent months of my dad's decline, we spent many hours together, and in the quiet of even pain-filled moments, he felt safe, allowing me to care for him, an honor, considering there is no better person and caregiver than my mom, who because of her steadfast grace, love and devotion, carried and nurtured my father through many illnesses. With Dad's passing breath came the deep loss of my own . . . each moment since his passing, I grasp hold of the strength he guided me with, and that's how he'd want it to be. For me and my dad, there will never be a place and time when we're not together. Although physical presence does not allow for that now, he's so much a part of me I won't know how to be otherwise . . ."

I knew my reverence would not stop following my speech but would take place in the now hushed and private space of my heart. I'm blessed with everything in my life, but the invaluable blessing I'm thankful for is the complete lack of regrets I have because I always let my father know how much I adored him.

Quiet Darkness

The hand that life deals us can be quite miraculous in its pain and joy. Once my father died, I did what I always do best: take care of others. It was literally the only way I knew how to take care of myself and move through my overwhelming grief and loss. I became laser-focused on helping my mom. Prior to the pandemic, my father had reached for my hand, and through choked breaths, uttered "Take care of Mom."

Always his reliable little soldier, I replied, "I will, Dad. I promise." Even without his asking, it would still have been number one on my radar. There was no way I could remove, repair, and assuage my mother's insurmountable grief and loss, which she was drowning in, but I would do everything in my power to alleviate what I could. I would spend the coming year reselling father's fine, beloved clothing collection (I'm certain somewhere he's bitching about getting $12 dollars for a $65 dollar belt), delivering meals, calling and FaceTiming twice daily, shipping puzzles, books and activities to the house, and visiting on the patio or in the garage when the pandemic was in full swing. In my mother's words, I became a lifeline, and for that, I was beyond grateful. To know that I helped my mother made me infinitely happy.

I would have done anything for her. The fact that helping her helped me was frosting on the cake.

My sister and her family were incredible. They delivered food and assisted with necessary administrative issues, household projects, and outside visits. Michael and his family in Colorado called and sent puzzles (Mom became very good at jigsaw puzzles!). We were all looking out for Mom and knew somewhere, Dad was looking down with a grateful heart, knowing she was well cared for.

Never during the pandemic, which coincided with our grief process, was anyone permitted access to my parents' house. Visits were under the cover of the garage or on the back patio. We had not felt the warmth of hugs, kisses, or touch. This highly unnatural separation was incredibly foreign at a time that begged for hyper connectedness, a life raft through the grieving process for all involved. Sadly, this experience is one so many people have endured during the pandemic.

In the Jewish religion, a Shiva takes place at the home of the deceased loved one. Due to the pandemic, gatherings were not permitted, and so, in the 102-degree heat of the day, on my mother's patio, in Scottsdale, Arizona, two grandchildren, two children, and two spouses gathered, flanked by an enormous swamp cooler, covered in face masks, six feet apart. Already at a loss of air due to grief, and barely able to breathe because of the heat and masks, the devastating loss, collectively dripped down our temples and from our eyes as we quietly ate lunch.

Family and friends provided us with food deliveries. In times of joy and grief, there is always food! How was I expected to get food down my throat when all I was swallowing was the salt of my sorrow?

The necessary logistics were discussed and somehow the day progressed like any other. How could the weight of a life not cause the world to come to a screeching halt? Yet nothing changed. The sun rose and set, the heat prevailed, and neighborhood dogs barked. It was all the same and yet, not. Here was a day without my father, our father, Mom's husband, the grandkids' grandfather, and the in-laws' father-in-law. A friend, a mentor, a life that held so much presence that it was profoundly palpable in his absence. Once allowed inside the house, I would find myself gazing at the dent he had made in the corner of the couch. As time would pass, the air around his forever seat seemed to thin in the lightness of his absence.

As I embarked on a mission to be a "tower of power" for my mother's healing, I quietly dealt with my own. The quiet darkness of the morning would find me awakened by warm tears streaming down my face. In the dim-lit start to each new day, I lay filled with profound sadness and emptiness. Choked with loss and privately shattered, I walked through my days. Then months. I adorned my environment with photos, knickknacks, and reminders of my father. I punctuated my world with pieces of my father.

As my mother finalized her cleaning out of Dad's shirts and pants, my guest room closet became the lair for his unsold belongings. Each time I opened the closet door, a waft of my father's essence spilled out, fragrant and bittersweet. Oh, my god, I could feel him there. How could it be that in the unpalatable act of liquidating his wardrobe, I found him? Over and over, I would find myself drawing open the closet doors if only for a second to close my eyes and smell the last vestiges I had of my father. This olfactory gift made me feel as if I could be with him again, if only for a few more times until his last shirt was gone.

I have always been a person who handles challenges on her own, and this would be no different. In the privacy of my heart, in solitary moments stolen during the day—driving, waking, falling asleep, in the shower, exercising on the elliptical—I nurtured and navigated my own pain. And so, as I have done many times in my life, I became my own rock even though there were moments in which it felt like I couldn't breathe, which was most of the time. My husband was an incredible source of strength and empathy, and I found comfort in his acceptance of my pained silence. I felt like an emotional astronaut, blackness surrounding me, untethered from the only base station that got me. Got me in silence, in laughter and in moments where sitting beside him made me feel supremely content. I reached out into the vast emptiness for my father's hand to pull me back and make everything OK. Floating in the ether of loss, I had to get a grip to return, where I knew he'd want me to be, even though it meant it would now be without him. Never had anyone with so few words said and done so much as my father had for me. Thinking wry Dad thoughts, I knew I'd need a trip to the hardware store to get a really long extension cord for what was to be our continued connection. I wouldn't haven't it any other way.

Andrea and I, tightly connected before, were now melded together, our mutual ache threading the needle of our shared experience. We checked on each other, recounted events and cried. Michael called to check on us, check on Mom and be of support in any way he could. As the only male in the family, often the mere timbre of his voice would bring me to tears unbeknownst to him. Distance prohibited me laying my head on his shoulder as I had on Dad's, yet I longed to do so. I was tired and just needed a little strength that came from someone other than me. I longed for one of my dad's wry quips to ease the pain just a little bit. I knew they would come. They always had and always would.

Incoming One-Liners

There is no question I miss my father with all my being every moment of every day. Yet, he feels so much a part of me that often I feel like he's walking with me throughout my daily interactions. So much so, it's as if he's resting somewhere in peaceful eternity with a megaphone, firing off one-liners at times when tears seem more appropriate. My father and I had so much comedic connection, that I now feel his post-mortem comedic commentaries in my head. My family has also perfected my father's facial contortions as well.

Since my father's passing, there have been many painfully piercing moments that began with a lump in my throat and culminated in quiet laughter bubbling up from my chest. Each time I quietly thank my father for inspiring a laugh.

The first New Year's following my dad's passing, I paid a visit to his "place" at the cemetery. It was my first new year without a dad. With emotion trapped in my throat, I softly approached my father's sparsely marked gravesite. In the Jewish religion, it's customary to undergo a stone setting ceremony one year following the death of a loved one. At the stone setting, the loved one's stone is unveiled for the family in a private graveside ceremony. Because we live in a kiln (a.k.a. Arizona), the heat would be unbearable in June, so my father's stone setting took place on April 18, 2021, instead. The family knew with great certainty Dad wouldn't want us "sweating our asses off." Until the stone setting, his life was demarcated by a 3x5 index card with his name, date of death, and internment. I couldn't help thinking that so much pertinent information was missing from that small white card.

Incoming one-liner: "Nice, this is what I get for 85 years of suffering: a freaking index card? Too bad they couldn't make it smaller, like on match book. That way the family could have an even harder time finding me than they do now!"

And just like that, my tears evaporated in the Arizona morning sun, and I began to chuckle. I gazed upward, unsure of where to extend my gratitude to my father for his help.

What do you say when you visit a deceased loved one at their place of rest? I felt odd speaking to grass. Yet, I felt I must say something, just in case he could hear. Quietly I uttered, "Happy New Year, Dad."

Incoming oneliner: "Yeah, it's happy. Me and all these dead people are hanging out celebrating the new year. Glad you found me this time. If the bird hadn't taken a shit on my postage stamp name marker, it could have been weeks!"

Another upward glance to share my gratitude for my father's gift of humor.

I was considering bringing flowers to place on his gravesite, but when I went to the store to select the perfect arrangement, all I could hear was:

Incoming oneliner: "Do me a favor, I hate flowers. If you want to do something nice, I'd rather have my horse poop next to my headstone."

One Year Later, Here's What I Know

It's been one year since my father died. Here's what I know. I know you can walk through grief and get to the other side. The grief doesn't go away; you go with the grief. Each step forward is a little farther from the piercing pain and a little closer to the fond memories. I know that everything will not be OK because that's life and that's death and that's what my father taught me. My father's humor was his personal tour guide through life. It saw him through his childhood, business dealings, and friendships, family life, pain, and ultimately the knowledge of his passing. He could turn pain on its end and flip it into laughter. He could turn fear into jabs and pierce his own bubble of nerves.

My father raised three amazing humans, giving, loving, loyal, intelligent, and all bound together by the love he and my mother created. My father was so very proud of my sister, the life she made for herself, and for her incredible strength. He knew he could always count on her. Michael was my father's brilliant sidekick. They shared business dealings, laughter, and travel, and dad was beyond proud of all that Michael accomplished and his beautiful family.

And then there was my mother. My father adored her. A man of few words, the commitment of more than sixty years together spoke volumes as a testament of his undying love for her. Through sickness and in health, truly they were yin and yang for the long haul. Theirs was a connection that ran so deep, it defied explanation and needed none. They got each other.

I'll forever be grateful and honored that my father's energy poured through me as a conduit of his passage to peace and comfort and back to his mother, sister, and brother, whom he loved dearly.

The day before my father passed away, I longed to hold his hand one last time. His skin was cool to the touch and his grip unresponsive. I softly slipped my hand in his, hoping for a squeeze, or slight response. Nothing came. He knew I was there, but was so far away, he was unable to let me know. It was enough to have the gift of his hand in mine. I took a photo of that moment, so I would forever be able to capture a visual of our bigger-than-life connection. From childhood to adulthood, I always adored holding his hand.

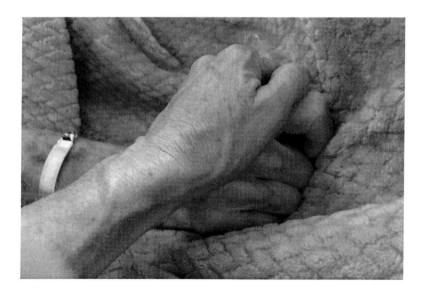

My siblings and I may have experienced our father differently, but each connection he had with his children was so very special to him. He was proud of his kids and each of us gleaned something different from him, making each connection no less impactful than the other. In the greatest of ironies, he may have been mercurial, critical, and filled with rules, but he definitely "got it right" in terms of the final passage in his life script that he so longed for. In perpetuity, he could now erase any irrelevant parental tapes of his father telling him he did something wrong.

My father said to my mother during one of my visits to their house, "Joan, I don't know what she weighs, but I'm sure it's all heart." As soon as I arrived home, I wrote down his words and never forgot them. Every so often, his emotions would erupt in the most glorious and impactful morsels.

I know the butterflies that I felt each time my father lovingly glanced at me have flown. But I also know a single one is left behind. It flits its wings when I see photos of my father. I feel a tickle in my heart when I hear his voice in my head.

One Year and Four Weeks, But Who's Counting?

It's July 22, 2021. It's been one year and four weeks since my father's passing. In actuality, it's the culmination of two years of counting. The counting began at the outset of his decline. It is not only in loss that we tick off days and hours but in the very anticipation of loss.

Steeped in the beginning of his end, as my father's illness progressed, his life was marked by counting and monitoring. How many Ensures did he consume, how many doctor's appointments did he attend, and what was the outcome of his blood work? How many hours did he sleep, how many times did he call, and how many parts of our lives were diminished because of his inability to be present?

Everyone was counting. Counting became coping. Somehow, each day would provide a formulaic calculation for what was to come, or how much longer he had. Even hospice was counting. Breaths, pulses, and other vitals. We counted along with hospice looking for answers to questions that essentially answered themselves.

Down to my father's very last moments of life, we were forced to count his respiration to determine if he was no longer with us, as his breathing was erratic and at moments it seemed he was gone but was not. Andrea and I sat beside my father and waited one last time, hoping we had something more to count. No breath came.

My father passed at 7:01 pm on June 22, 2020. Immediately, as if not already bone tired from tallying moments prior to his death, I began counting how many minutes have passed since my father left me. In the span of one minute, the tear in my insides is so deep, it's unthinkable. With all the counting and emotional logging of his life, there was nothing left to count. And now, the very man I counted on my entire life is gone. I counted on his evergreen presence; I counted on his warm shoulder, on his laughter, his hugs and his unconditional love for me. I counted on him being witness to my life. I can no longer count on the act of counting, the life raft that kept hope afloat. He is gone.

In these first moments without my father, I can hear his voice telling me once again, "Deena, you can't tell someone that everything will be OK, because it's not. It's not going to be OK." And I wasn't, Mom wasn't, Andrea wasn't, Michael wasn't. None of my father's kids, spouses, grandkids were OK. We are heartbroken and lost.

Through the unnatural separation caused by the pandemic, through a year's worth of holidays, firsts, administrative tasks related to his death, and just pure grieving, a year came and went.

It's July 22, 2021. Not only is it a year and four weeks since my father died, but it's my mother's 85th birthday. In my home, the adult children gather around my mother at the dinner table to celebrate her milestone. As I sit at the table surrounded by my family, now gathered for the first time since my father's passing, I'm keenly aware of both my father's absence and his presence.

My father's absence is keenly felt in the places in our home where he would regularly roost. I feel his absence from his designated seat at the table, his quips, stories, and bearing witness to everything the family did and experienced. Whether I was showing him my new car, or he was sitting with me as I recovered from a surgery, my father was always a witness to my life. Life was somehow validated if you could share it with my father.

Michael shares moving and funny stories. We laugh and allow space for feeling each experience. It's beautiful, sad, and a testament to his legacy.

As I scan the table taking in the safe circle of our family, I know things will never be the same. Over and over, my father's words ring in my ears, "Things are not going to be OK, Deena." I understand his words and feelings to be true. But I also understand the strength of the souls seated at the table. I realized we would be OK in a different way. A new way.

I've learned to live with the loss. I'm a new version of myself and have found an OK place. In classic Deena fashion, I'll push the envelope and be fearless to the deep pain and loss I'm experiencing. I'll laugh through it, cry through it, paint through it, and move through it.

Some days the flowers look the way they did before I lost my father, but then without warning, a Mack truck of emotion washes over me. Like a ghost in Harry Potter's library, I allow the feelings to pass through me.

There will never be a new wallet or purse I won't anxiously await my father's reach into his pocket for a crisp dollar bill to "bless" it with.

There will never be a warm shoulder, on the corner most part of the purple couch, to lay my head on and a rough hand to cup my chin and smile at me with all the love in the world.

I cannot drive a new car over to show you, or tell you how our businesses is doing when you ask, "You make any sales today?" There are no feet to sit by, no warm hands to hold, no pop-overs to bring you a sub. There is no "you" anymore.

Exhausted from counting and hypervigilance, after a year, I believe my counting has come to a much-needed rest. So, I did the only thing I knew how to do, one last time. I counted on the strength my father gave me to help me move forward. To help me help my mom. To help me be there for my husband, daughter, brother, and sister, and to help me heal the most painful experience of my life.

"Everything is not OK, Dad, but it will get better. It's getting better. It's not OK. It's just different."

I never feel alone. My father is always with me. And on this hot, summer evening on July 22, 2021, in my backyard, as I have many nights since his passing, I gaze up toward the sky, searching out the star that is my father and think, *OK, Little Bird. You got this.*

Incoming Oneliner: "Well that's nice, Deena. So now you think of me when you're standing in the yard with all the dog poop?"

"Daaaad!"

Acknowledgements

When my father uttered, "OK, Little Bird" weeks before he passed, I knew something inside me had changed. I also knew, it was the beginning of the most painful and rewarding experience of my life – the writing of this memoir. As if loss and grief weren't enough to handle, all this transpired at the height of the Covid19 pandemic. I literally "masked" my pain.

As my father's spark dimmed two days prior to dying, my spark ignited. I became a locomotive of determination to capture and document 57 years' worth of life with my father, and the hilarious, unique, and deep connection we shared. Along the way I barreled through painful loss and heartache. Once I completed writing the memoir, I knew this "Little Bird" would be OK.

Editorial assistance was needed to bring this baby to fruition. I was specific in my desire to find someone who had an amazing sense of humor, who got my humor, and who would be unfazed by the world of my father's unfiltered comments. Most importantly, someone who saw past my father's grumble and felt the incredible bond we shared.

That incredible person is my editor, Holly Rubino, who I'm endlessly grateful for. Your expertise, talent, humor, and incredible responsiveness to my 4:00am emails were unparalleled. You gave "Little Bird" the wings it needed to soar, and for that, there is not enough chocolate in the universe to thank you properly.

To my incredibly loving and supportive husband, Sandy, who sat through countless hours of listening and sharing. I have endless love for my mother, sister, and brother, who provided me with anecdotes, facts, and a little advice along the way. Your contributions to the accuracy of my memory were much needed. Your love, support and impact in my life are immeasurable.

To my daughter Lindy, I've poured all the love and joy I was given as a child, into raising and adoring you. I hope you feel it. I hope it's a source of strength and light in your life. Know that humor and strength will see you through everything in yours.

To my father's grandkids, Taryn, Matt, Jason, Jacqueline, and Lindy. You are grandpa's legacy of love and humor. He was beyond proud of each of you for your unique strengths and gifts, and he loved you dearly. To spouse-in-laws, Sandy, Lee, and Abby – dad welcomed you into the familial fold and loved you for making each of his children fulfilled, cared for and happy and for the special people you are and the unique connections you each shared with him.

I thank my friends for their patience and support as I passed on social events, get- togethers and staying in touch while my world was illuminated by the light of my laptop for weeks on end.

And finally, to dad, sorry you had to be "out of town" when our story was published. I'm pretty sure you wanted to be here but know somewhere in the ether you are checking the calendar to see if you are "available" to read and discuss. Either way, you are in my heart forever!